Develop Your ESP

Develop Your ESP

A Quick and Easy Way to Become Psychic

Nina Ashby

A Sterling / Zambezi Book

Sterling Publishing Co., Inc.

New York

Library of Congress Cataloging-in-Publication Data Available

2   4   6   8   10   9   7   5   3   1

Published in 2004 by
Sterling Publishing Co., Inc.
387 Park Avenue South
New York, NY 10016

Copyright © 2004 Nina Ashby
Cover design: © 2004

Published and distributed in the UK soley by
Zambezi Publishing Limited
P.O. Box 221 Plymouth,
Devon PL2 2YJ (UK)

Distributed in Canada by Sterling Publishing
$^{c}/o$ Canadian Manda Group
165 Dufferin Street
Toronto, Ontario, Canada M6K 3H6

Distributed in Australia by Capricorn Link (Australia) Pty Ltd.
P.O. Box 704, Windsor, NSW 2756, Australia

Typesetting by Zambezi Publishing, Plymouth UK

Manufactured in the USA
All rights reserved.

Sterling ISBN 1-4027-1220-0
Zambezi ISBN 1-903065-30-5

Acknowledgments

Psychics have told me for the past twenty five years that I should be writing and I have finally made it happen! I wish to thank Sasha and Jan for providing the impetus and opportunity to write this book; their positive encouragement and belief in my abilities is deeply appreciated.

Thanks also to all the students who, over the years, have helped me to gain more understanding. They provided the necessity to structure these insights in a cogent way and, therefore, have all contributed in their own right. Special thanks to Gordana Maric, Kathy Cazana, Nicole Curtis Salamate, Megan Patel, and Julia Nix for allowing me to use their experiences as examples.

Much appreciation is due to my mother for her patience and organizational ability, and for supplying me with the computer and space to write the bulk of this book. Thanks to my brother, Philip, for the use of his luxury "view corridor." Last, but definitely not least, a huge thanks is also due to my husband, Douglas, for his belief in me, his critical eye, his editing skills, his constant encouragement, and his unstinting support.

Contents

1

You Are Psychic

Our normal perception of the world around us is based on our five physical senses of sight, hearing, touch, taste, and smell. The messages that we receive from these sources are conveyed to the brain, where we process them and then relate them to past experiences that are stored in our memory. We then come to a decision about what we perceive and act or react accordingly. We are not conscious of this process most of the time, because it happens so quickly that we do not stop and consider it; we just know what we are experiencing.

From time to time we find ourselves "knowing" something that does not seem to have anything to do with rational physical perception. Call it what you want: sensitivity, intuition, a hunch, a feeling, or extra sensory perception (ESP). It is this elusive "knowing" that gives us information, motivation, and direction at odd times in your life. It can be about any aspect of our lives: personal, professional, or some other context. Often the impression that we receive is so subtle and fleeting that we dismiss it as our imagination—and even when events prove us to be right, it gets rejected as being coincidence. We are all born with this subtle side of our nature, with the ability to perceive beyond our five physical senses. It is part of the fabric of our physical and supraphysical being.

I use the word *subtle* in this book to mean something that is not obvious. Thus a subtle experience or matter relates to those things that blend into or emerge from our psychic, inner, intuitive, or "auric" experience —as opposed to those things that are obvious and that are part of our normal daily lives.

Some people seem to be born with the ability to be more closely in touch with this subtle aspect of existence, just as some are born with musical, athletic, or artistic gifts. Many who are like this are either fascinated or fearful about their gifts, though there are also those who simply accept them as being part of the way in which they perceive the world, even to the extent of believing that everyone else perceives things the way they do. As with any talent, intuition needs to be developed in order to use it properly. One must also learn to use it responsibly and with understanding and compassion. We all have this extrasensory or physical aspect, and we all have the potential to be psychic. It is a question of acceptance—and of making the effort to understand and develop a conscious relationship with the more subtle aspects of who and what we are.

Coincidence or Psychic Reality?

Have you ever heard the telephone ring and just known who is on the other end before they spoke?

Have you suddenly thought of someone with whom you have not been in touch for a long time, shortly before they called you?

Have you asked about someone in passing, and that person calls without knowing that you had asked?

Have you received a letter out of the blue from someone
with whom you have not been in touch for ages,
soon after you have been thinking of them?

Have you walked down the street, and, for no particular
reason, found someone on your mind—and then
they suddenly appear?

Have you driven along a road, then felt that you needed
to turn in a particular direction, even though it is
not your usual route, and then discovered there
was a traffic jam on your normal route that would
have held you up?

Have you dreamed something about someone or about an
event that proves to be true?

Have you walked into a place for the first time and
picked up "bad vibes" about it, only to discover
later that an upsetting event, a tragedy, or some
terrible thing had taken place there?

Have you sat next to someone and begun to have
sensations such as aches or pains that you do not
normally experience, only for the person to tell
you that they experience those aches and pains?

Have you had a gut feeling about someone or something
that eventually proves to be true, even though it is
not immediately apparent?

Have you ever felt uncomfortable in the presence of a
stranger for no apparent reason, only to discover
later that the person was unpleasant, untrustworthy,
or unbalanced in some way?

This is a small list of common occurrences that I have
experienced, as have my friends, clients, and students.
You have probably had one or more of these kinds of
things happen to you, too—and this is not a coincidence!
This is because our physical and subtle senses are at
work all the time. The problem is that we are so used to
receiving and acting on what we perceive by our five

conscious senses that most of these inner messages get drowned out or ignored because we can see no physical basis for believing them. Therefore, some of the first things we have to learn are to *listen*, to be *open,* and to be *receptive* to what our subtle senses are telling us. However, before we embark on this, there are some other things we need to look at first.

In the course of my work as a teacher, therapist, and psychic reader, I have met many people who are naturally receptive to those subtle levels of being. They receive impressions about events or other people, but do not know what to do with them, and they cannot work out if their impressions are real or just figments of their imagination. Many are frightened by their ability to see or hear inwardly or to feel the emotions or physical sensations that others feel, and they would rather that this ability just went away. On more than one occasion I have been asked "Can't you just make it stop?" The answer is that you cannot, any more than you can or should want to get rid of any one of your physical senses. What you *can* do is to learn to control this ability and put it to good use rather than being overwhelmed by it. That is one of the purposes of this book—to show you how to do this. Many of the techniques and exercises that can help you develop your innate psychic, extrasensory ability can also be turned around so that you learn to develop conscious control over it.

Information Processing

Some of the most frequently asked questions I get as a teacher of psychic development have to do with information processing:

> Where does the information come from?
> What do I do with that information?

How do I know if there is any truth in it?
Is it real or just my imagination?
Did I unknowingly make it up?
If they are messages, where are they coming
     from?
Should I share my ideas with anyone else—and if
     I do, what will they think?
Is the information symbolic or literal?

Everything that you experience in your daily life is recorded within your astral databanks. What you are *aware of* becomes dependent upon the filters that you have developed to help you process information. In psychic development work, you seek to expand your filters, allowing you to comfortably access and process more than the normal range of information that you receive. Along this route, you need to sharpen all your senses and begin to validate the information that you receive in this subtle manner. You also need to become brave enough to speak up about your experiences and expose them to the light of day. This will help you discern what is real and what is not—and it builds confidence.

So—why do these weird and wonderful things happen—and how?

Where Does the Information Come From?
Obviously some of it comes from the world outside of you—from places and people. It also comes from within. Your intelligence is the means of obtaining, distributing, and manipulating information, and this operates within your various subtle layers. Sometimes a part of your subconscious mind seeks information from your memory banks that is not readily available in your current consciousness file. Then it conveys it to you through thought, imagery, emotional feeling, or sensations.

How Can I Tell My Higher Self From My Lower Self?

"What do you mean when you say that I have two selves?" We have two separate vehicles for dealing with information—our "lower self" and our "higher self."

Our *lower self* handles day-to-day matters of survival and it is particularly involved with list making. It is characteristically busy, noisy, and repetitive. In this case, *lower* does not mean *lesser* but *denser* or that part of ourselves which deals with physical, practical matters. We need this self to keep us organized and on track in the physical plane.

Our *higher self* handles more subtle information. It has the whole "back files" of our astral databank from which to draw, as well as intimations of our soulic experiences. Our higher self is not necessarily better, but it is less dense and it has a wider perspective. It is characteristically slow, quiet, and unobtrusive. Information that comes in through this route may be repeated only once or twice if we are lucky. It is the level on which we seek inner answers and to reaffirm our relationship with our center.

Which Station Do You Tune Into the Most?

Perception is a complex and fascinating process. In a manner similar to the way in which our physical senses function, our subtle senses pick up information in different channels or frequency bands, rather like radio signals. When stimulated, they record and process information; and then communicate it appropriately through something called the chakra system. We will examine this system in some detail later, but for the moment it is sufficient to know that while each chakra works in itself, it is also in touch with all of the others, so that information is circulated through the system at lightening speed. We process information visually, aurally, and kinesthetically, and we switch back and forth between these access modes.

Everyone has one or two physical senses that are dominant, and that they rely on most. The same tends to be true of our subtle senses, or the frequency "bands" that can be used when receiving and processing information. We also use the other bands but we are simply less aware of them.

Everybody has psychic ability, some are more in touch with their ability than others. Trained psychics simply pay more attention to their inner world. They are able to have better control over their energies and they are aware of how they use these energies through communication and action in the world. In this way they are better able to filter more information in the context of life and then reflect it back to others. I suppose you could say we have bigger "psychic muscles" than other folk and can thus keep our attention focused for longer periods of time at the different layers of energy.

I am not of the school of thought that says that in order to become psychic you simply need to learn to open up and see what comes in, or that if you are a natural psychic you do not need training. In order to use any ability proficiently you need to undertake training of some kind. I have been psychic and able to see auras since childhood, and my understanding and ability to use my gifts in the way I do now has only come about through many years of training. I have had to develop breathing and energy skills, meditation, interpretation, and expressive skills. Creating habitual structures for "tuning in," structuring the course of the reading, asking inner questions, and "tuning out" are essential elements for any student to learn in order to progress in their inner work. In my view, these are indispensable for professional practice.

In this book I will deal with all these things in detail and provide you with exercises that you can use to develop your own particular psychic abilities. An understanding of how these abilities function is crucial to safe and effective psychic work, so be prepared to tackle the more theoretical bits as well as the practical work that you will encounter. As you do the exercises, the theory will become clear. Before we move on to these, there are some questions that arise quite regularly in connection with being psychic that we should deal with now.

Spirituality, Religion and Psychic Matters

Spirituality pertains to sacred, unworldly, nonmaterial aspects of existence. Humanity has always sought to define its relationship with nature and the unseen world, seeking in the process to understand the nature of existence. Our need to celebrate this relationship and bring us closer to the source of order in the universe has lead to the development and existence of many philosophies and religions down the ages. Religions have different views about psychic matters. In the past (and still, for some), religions embraced human psychic nature, and the schools of teaching associated with them have taught people how to develop psychic abilities and use them in a spiritual context. Many of today's religions reject anything psychic, warning against the use of such "powers" and of predicting the future. In some instances certain of their adherents go so far as to see anything psychic as being evil. This is rather sad in my view, for it prevents these people from being able to experience the inner realities of their own religion in a way that is only open to those who have developed their inner psychic perception. Having taken part in several religious movements during the course of my own spiritual development, I have experienced this through clairvoyant observation of their inner workings. These phenomena have little to do with the dogma of various religious teachings, but a great deal to do with the spiritual essence that is their true foundation. It is true that the line between the use of any kind of knowledge for good or evil can be very thin. Therefore, an important part of learning about psychic matters does focus on moral and ethical considerations in addition to the need for great responsibility in how that extended awareness is used in the world.

Destiny or Free Will?

This is an important, age-old question to consider. I believe that we have a destiny that is contained within our pattern of incarnation. Our destiny constitutes the strengths and abilities that help us to overcome the weaknesses and the challenges we must meet for our learning experience in the current lifetime. It determines some of the significant people whom we will meet as well as certain situations that we must face during the course of our lifetime. The pattern also defines the genetic and socioeconomic background into which we appear in this life, which affects our outlook.

Free will represents the ability to choose how we act. This has to be in consciousness—in other words, beyond the habitual reactions that stem from our pattern. The frictions, difficult decisions, and pain we go through in life are often the result of the battle between the "shoulds"—learned behaviors designed to please others—and our deepest sense of what is right for us. The ability to develop insight and to have the courage to recognize and act upon what is right for us relates to the use of free will to meet our destiny and to develop wisdom.

Why Go to a Psychic Reader?

People have readings for many different reasons. Some have a problem to solve or feel lost, confused, and out of control. Others just want to see the pattern of what will present itself during the coming year or period that is ahead. Going for a reading or doing one for yourself helps you to obtain an overview of your current life circumstances. Insight encourages you to see more than one possible choice of action for the future. Action often has to do with outlook, so when you change your perspective on a situation, you can alter what you end up doing about it. This way you cease to be a victim and learn to take real responsibility for your actions rather than just react to situations.

For example: Peter was a client who is self-employed. When I looked at his work and money matters for the year ahead, I could see a time period of three months coming up when his income would not be good. The time preceding it was very good, and afterward it would suddenly be strong again. I advised him to be prepared and to put money aside during the preceding time in order to tide him over during the slow period. I also reassured him that it would last only for this short duration. Instead of being anxious, he could then plan ahead, relax and use the slow time to concentrate on other projects, catch up on a backlog of work, and take some time off before things became busy again.

Predictions

How can psychics make predictions? We all make predictions during the course of our daily lives. These are based on what we know from previous experiences, which helps us in our decision-making. We are also creatures of habit. In other words, our habits create patterns that you can read or that can be read by others who are capable of observing them. Where we are today stems from the decisions we have made in the past. These include the ways in which we have dealt with the various kinds of life experiences that we have already encountered.

Likewise, the choices we make now will have an effect on how our future will develop. Just as an invisible thought precedes a visible action, so events that will come to pass within the physical world are foreshadowed within the subtle worlds. By using psychic perception, psychic readers obtain information about these events and pass it on to their clients. Psychic predictions then tend to be a combination of reading the pattern of past, present, and future as laid down by the individual through his own decisions and actions, thus perceiving specific events that lie in the life pathway for that person.

2

Our Subtle Selves

We are more than just a physical body. All esoteric teachings down the ages have affirmed this; so do all those religions that believe in some form of life after death, and in the existence of some aspect of our selves that is variously called the soul or spirit. Science tells us that everything in the universe is a form of energy, and that matter in its various states is simply energy locked up in form. Another key concept in both esoteric teachings and in modern physics has to do with vibration. In this view of the universe, visible and invisible, measurable and as yet immeasurable— everything can be conceived of as being part of a cosmic keyboard upon which all things have their place according to their rate of vibration. Sound, radio waves, heat, light, cosmic radiation—all have their place on the cosmic keyboard, and so do our subtle energy bodily systems. Because they function at vibratory rates beyond anything that we can detect or measure with physical instruments, we have to rely on psychic observation for our understanding of them.

There are a number of ways in which the various aspects of our total being are represented in esoteric teachings. The difference between them stems mainly from the different perspective that is being taken. For example, one fourfold division sees the physical body as being the vehicle through which the "personality self" manifests. This in turn is the vehicle through which the soul can function—the soul itself being the vehicle of manifestation for our eternal "spirit." The "personality self" has both emotional and mental aspects to it. A more useful representation of psychic matters has come down to us from Eastern teachings, particularly the yoga tradition. This is the chakra system.

Chakra is a Sanskrit word meaning "wheel," and this describes the movement of energy with a center. In fact, each chakra is an energy vortex that spins at a different rate. Chakras act as transformers that transmute energies up and down the vibrational frequency bands, and they are linked to the physical body via the nervous system in association with nerve plexuses as well as with the endocrine system. The endocrine glands secrete hormones that control all biochemical processes of the body. In other words, bodies are layered: each layer has its own particular structure and function. The layers are interpenetrated by the chakras that allow them to communicate with one another by circulating energies up and down the planes.

Your Energy Bodies

Your physical body is the densest aspect of your energy field. Most people see their physical body as emitting their energy field. However, I believe it is actually the other way around—that the body is our life energy's final manifestation into the physical plane. For me, the physical plane is very much a development of the spiritual world.

Our physical body is primarily a biochemical factory that is thermal in nature. Our subtle bodies vary in structure and they function according to the

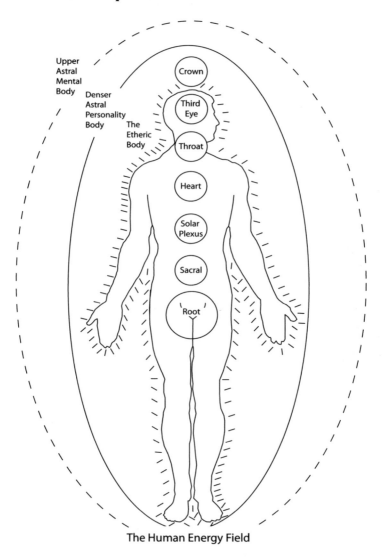

The Human Energy Field

vibrational frequency band in which they operate. They are governed by the laws pertaining to that band or "plane." The interface between our subtle structures and our physical body lies within our chakra system.

The Etheric Body

This, the densest of the subtle fields, is our electromagnetic body. It exists within and around every cell, emanating three to five inches around the physical body. It has been called the etheric double, as it provides the template for the structures of the physical body.

Everyone's etheric body is unique. It is made up of tiny hairlike structures that store electromagnetic vitality. These structures are apparent on Kirlian photographs, a method of imagery developed by the Russian scientist Semyon Kirlian in Russia in 1939. To produce Kirlian photographs, a high voltage, low amperage current is brought into contact with the body, which is then exposed to a photographic plate. You will notice the feathery, hairlike emanations. The stronger the person's vitality, the more profuse and longer the structures. These structures are hollow and they store vitality. This imparts either the glow of health around a vigorous person or the opposite state of when someone is lackluster. A healthy animal's fur is fluffy, glossy and often full of static electricity, while an ailing animal's fur is matted and limp. The etheric field can be seen with the

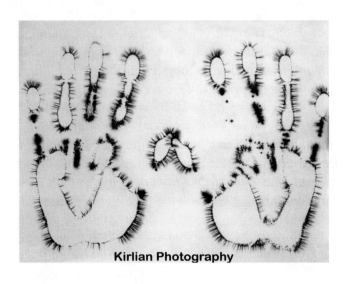

Kirlian Photography

human eye, appearing as a colorless glow around a person, very much like heat rising from a radiator.

Aside from storing vitality, the etheric body circulates energy via pathways known within the Eastern traditions as *meridians*. One could think of them as roadways, major thoroughfares, secondary roads, side streets, and traffic circles. These pathways interface with our skin as points of greater electrical resistance. In the Chinese tradition these are the acupuncture points, and in the Japanese tradition they are called *tsubos*. Stimulating these points in a systematic manner treats physical systemic problems as well emotional, mental, and spiritual difficulties, thus striving to bring vitality and harmonious function to the etheric system.

The etheric exists in plants and animals too. Kirlian photographs show that if you take a photograph of a whole leaf, its etheric field glows around it. When you cut the leaf in half, the etheric glow persists in the same space that the actual leaf occupied prior to cutting, and it continues to do so over a period of time. This can be likened to "phantom limb syndrome" where, post-amputation, the person still feels sensations relating to the missing body part at a distance from the remaining physical body.

Facts—the Etheric Body:
> Template for the physical body.
> Extends three to five inches beyond the skin.
> Stores vitality as electromagnetic energy.
> Energy circulated through meridians.
> Perceived as a colorless glow around body.

Becoming Aware of the Etheric Body
You can feel and see the etheric field easily! Here are some basic exercises for you to experiment with.

Exercise 1: Becoming Energy Aware

Relax and prepare yourself to become energy aware. Rub your hands together and hold them about six inches apart, palms facing each other. Close your eyes and breathe slowly and deeply, concentrating on the space between your palms for several minutes. You should begin to feel one or more of the following physical sensations: heat, tingling, magnetic attraction/repulsion, resistance, throbbing, pulsing. This is due to a build of vitality in the etheric field between your palms.

Once you feel the sensation(s), slowly draw your hands away from one another, being aware of how long the sensations continue. The sensation may be subtler but still present.

Exercise 2: Feeling Your Etheric Energy

Take both arms and raise them up straight in front of you. Notice if there is any difference in the sensation and ease of lifting your arms or in the feeling as they rest next to your sides.

Now, take your right hand and place it in the air about four inches above your left shoulder with the palm down. Slowly stroke down your left arm toward the top of your left hand. Remember to breathe and concentrate during this process. Repeat this five times. Stay aware of any sensations you may have.

When finished, raise your arms up straight in front of you again, noting any difference in sensation between them. If you feel the left arm to be heavier and slightly swollen, then you have felt the effects of manipulating the energies within the etheric field.

If you felt a warm, tingly, and/or pulsing sensation during the stroking, then you have come into contact with your etheric field. Try this with plants, animals, and other people, noting any differences in sensation.

Exercise 3: Seeing the Etheric Field.

The etheric appears as a colorless glow around people, animals, and plants. Some see it as a gray-blue mist. Remember that the more vitality the object has, the easier it will be to see its etheric field. In order to see it, you must use your eyes in a different way.

Get a friend to sit across the room from you. Now, keeping your eyes relaxed, look beyond your friend at head level, including the person within the field of your vision rather than focusing on any particular part of his body. You should see the glow near to the body.

Repeat this with other people, houseplants, trees (they have a much larger field than humans), or pets.

Spread your fingers against a dark background. Squint your eyes and look at the background, including your hands in the field. Relax your eyes and you will begin to see a colorless shimmering outline several inches around the fingers, like heat coming off a radiator.

The Astral Body

This is the largest of the fields surrounding your body. It comprises several distinct layers.

For the sake of convenience we can consider these under two headings, designated "upper and lower astral."

The densest or "lower astral" level relates to the *personality body*. This stores all its information in a swirling cloud of color. It emanates three to five feet

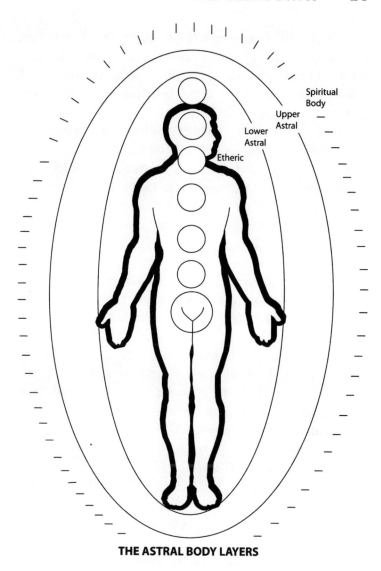

Spiritual
Body

Upper
Astral

Lower
Astral

Etheric

THE ASTRAL BODY LAYERS

from the physical body and is egg shaped. The personality body is the one we all "tune into" to sense someone's vibrations. This happens in all our interactions with others, not just when we are doing psychic work. Our personality is the combination of the life pattern we manifest at birth. It is reflected in and generated by our genetic structure and our life experiences. This "lower astral" level reflects our everyday emotional and mental states and we can equate it with that "lower self" that I spoke of in the previous chapter.

The "upper astral" level is subtler, so it relates more to the finer feelings, such as compassion and to our higher aspirations. It is the plane of mentation rather than just thought, of contemplation rather than analysis. Again we can relate this to the "higher self" that I mentioned earlier, or at least as the means whereby we can contact and bring through information from that aspect of ourselves.

Another way to relate to this is that the *denser astral part is your current filing cabinet* and the *second astral layer is the "back files."* These layers also contain your "astral databank" for this lifetime. All your life experiences are filed here in memory as *thought forms.* They can be pulled into the present from storage for use in all aspects of your life. Thought forms are images that are linked with thought and all the other sensory information of the moment.

Color and the Astral World

The world, both outer and inner, is full of color. Even blind people see inner color. We are "beings of light." Much spiritual literature speaks of God as "light." We could not exist on earth without the sun, and the cycles of our lives are governed by the solar cycle of light and darkness. The more deprived we are of solar light, the more our mental, emotional, and physical health deteriorates. Color is the interaction between darkness and light. The physical plane is crystallized light. The mineral world that dominates the construction of the physical plane is colored, as are all the vegetable and animal kingdoms.

Our inner world also is one of light and color. Try closing your eyes. Can you see colors against a dark field? They can be geometric patterns or images. Colors represent different aspects of energy.

Our astral body is our body of light, and it stores information as color. The dominant color of the denser astral aura, which filters and influences the colors that are manifest in the rest of the aura, represents the kind of person we are, as well as indicating the nature of our life pattern (see the chapter on color). This color does not change significantly throughout a person's life, and it shows the foundation of the soulic lessons that dominate someone's personal life. The individual chakra colors that we will deal with shortly represent how an individual is using his consciousness to deal with the challenges of living. The colors in the astral body near the chakras change more rapidly, and these relate to the near past or to the future, pertaining to the nature of the chakra in question.

People who can see astral color can learn to read how a person is living his life by the nature of his energy colors. Even if you cannot see the astral aura, you can also get lots of clues about a person's personality by the colors he consciously or unconsciously chooses to wear or have around him. There will be a lot more information about color and its application to psychic awareness as we proceed.

Facts—the Astral Body:

Lower Astral—vehicle for the emotional and lower mental bodies.

Upper Astral—vehicle for higher feelings and mental processes.

Extends three to five feet beyond the skin.

Stores life experiences as thought forms.

Swirling cloud of energy moving in spiral manner.

Perceived as a cloud of colors around the body.

Experiencing the Astral Body

In order to do these experiments, you must suspend your current belief (or disbelief) and remain open. Eventually, you will get results. There will be more development exercises later on to help you. Do not worry if you cannot feel or see anything. There are other ways to tune into the astral field.

Exercise 1: Feeling the Astral Field

Ask a friend to stand comfortably with his eyes closed.

Move about six feet away from him and face him. Shake your hands and relax. Put your hands, palms facing outward, at the level of your stomach. They are like a radar dish that can receive energy signals.

SLOWLY walk toward your friend while concentrating on the sensation in your hands. At some point you will feel a *subtle* tingling sensation in your palms or fingertips. You may even notice that your friend is beginning to sway. When this happens you will know that you are in contact with his astral boundary.

Once you have identified the boundary, use a patting motion and continue to sense the shape of the astral field.

Exercise 2. Seeing the Astral Field

It can be quite a shock to see subtle color that is different from the outer or inner light that you have already experienced. You must relax your eyes as you did in the etheric exercise, and seek to perceive the world as energy rather than physical and solid.

Sit across the room from a friend.
Look at the space behind him so that he is in the field of
   your vision. First have a sense of the energy of
   the space, and of your friend. You may be able to
   see the swirling energy, although you may not see
   it as color at first. Astral colors are faint and
   subtle.
You can also look about eight inches from the physical
   body, moving your eyes and scanning around.
If you see a color and then focus on it, it will disappear.
   Just relax your eyes again.

Try this with several people sitting across from you. First
take a good look at their physical complexion and other
physical aspects before beginning. Then sit back and relax,
adjust your eyes, and scan rapidly across from person to
person. Do you see any differences in their energies? Do
these differences relate to their complexions—or to
something else?

   Looking around the head is often the best place to
start. We can now move on to a consideration of the
chakra system and how it relates to these subtle energy
bodies.

Chakras

The word *chakra* is derived from the Sanskrit word,
meaning "wheel." The chakra wheels mirror the
rotational movement of energies that are contained
within each chakra. In the etheric body there are said to
be 72,000 chakras. Think of a traffic system—it is easy
to imagine that the etheric chakras are like traffic circles.
They spin in one direction only and act as energy shunts,
moving energy along the meridian lines that are the
roadways. Just as roads and traffic circles can be small or
large depending on the amount of traffic they carry, so

too with these etheric chakras and the meridians they serve.

There are seven major chakras placed along the center of the body, and these are what are commonly thought of when referring to the chakras. Operating in both the etheric and astral fields, these major chakras have an entirely different role to the purely etheric ones. They are multidimensional in nature and these translate energies between the energy bodies, stepping it up or down in frequency or vibrational rate, so that each can be used at the appropriate level. They are therefore considered to be centers of consciousness, and each chakra can rotate clockwise or counterclockwise or indeed in all directions simultaneously, albeit at different rates.

Each of these major centers is concerned with a certain area of life relating to physical, emotional, mental, and spiritual states. Each one governs an aspect of the physical body in association with an endocrine gland, the etheric body via the nervous system in association with a nerve plexus, and also the astral body via color. Knowing about the chakra functions in depth bestows a great understanding of an individual's physical, psychological, and spiritual state. It is essential in developing personal understanding, as well as the development of their healing and reading skills. A little work goes a long way when dealing with chakra energies!

For the purposes of symbolism, there is an association between the progression of rainbow colors and each chakra. However, any color can be normal when associated with a chakra, as it describes the energy being expressed in life of the person at that time. More on that later.

Let us now look at each center individually in a bit more depth.

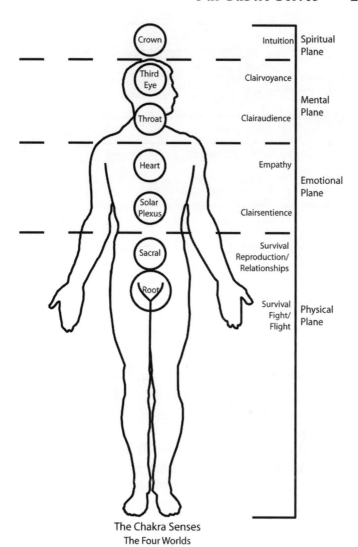

The Chakra Senses
The Four Worlds

THE ASSOCIATIONS			
CHAKRA	**ENDOCRINE GLAND**	**NERVE PLEXUS**	**COLOR**
Root	Adrenals	Anterior sacral	Red
Sacral	Gonads	Posterior sacral	Orange
Solar Plexus	Spleen & pancreas	Solar plexus	Yellow
Heart	Thymus	Cardiac	Green
Throat	Thyroid & parathyroid	Brachial	Turquoise
Third eye	Pituitary	Sympathetic	Indigo
Crown	Pineal	Parasympathetic	Violet

Root Center (I)

Location: This extends from just below the pubic bone to about halfway down the thighs. It has the slowest rate of rotation and it is concerned with our survival within the physical plane.

Governs: This center tells us about a person's current evolutionary cycle. Each cycle lasts for about two and a half years and relates to a specific set of learning experiences that the individual must pass through internally, and also through what he attracts externally.

Psychic function: Physical Plane. Survival.

Endocrine gland: Adrenal glands. Located above the kidneys in the mid back. The adrenal glands govern fight or flight reactivity for survival in the physical world. This is the only chakra where the endocrine gland is not directly over the chakra's actual physical zone.

Nerve plexus: Posterior sacral plexus. Governs the nerves of large intestine and is responsible for elimination of solid waste. The metaphor relates to eliminating things that are no longer useful, and thus of letting go.

Psychological: If you can see astral colors, then whatever colors are present in the chakra will offer a detailed description of the types of experiences that person is attracting. It also tells about the basic health constitution of the individual. If it is large, strong, and energetic, then the constitution is strong, but if it is weak, then the person is constitutionally vulnerable. The energy state also tells how "grounded" that person is.

Color: The color red bears a metaphorical relationship to this center because red represents pure energy. It is the lowest vibrational frequency of the spectrum and is hot, dense, and physical. It also represents the "fight or flight" response and nervous irritability. Too much red is over stimulating.

Keyword: Physical survival.

Sacral Center (We)

Location: Between the navel and the pubic bone.

Governs: Relationships.

Psychic function: Physical plane. Survival of the species through reproduction and social relationships.

Endocrine gland: Gonads—female ovaries and male testes. These glands assure the perpetuation of the species. They also define our biological being and influence our sociological functions and activities, from how we relate to ourselves to how others relate to us.

Nerve plexus: Anterior sacral plexus. This governs the generative organs as well as bladder function.

Psychological: How we manage ourselves in relationships is a key to personal growth and productivity in life. The center reflects how we relate to our gender identity and our ability to be practically creative in our daily lives. It also represents the ways in which we cope emotionally with the world and let go of emotional problems, as and when it is appropriate for us to do so.

Color: Orange. The color of ambition, politics and negotiation, appetite, and motivation.

Keyword: Relationships. Governs and reflects: firstly our relationship with our self and then the range of relationships that we have with others.

Solar Plexus Center (I will)

Location: The soft tissue over the stomach, just below the breastbone.

Governs: Decision-making.

Psychic function: Emotional plane. Clairsentience, which is the ability to feel clear sensations relating to subtle physical matter, like sensing ley lines and earth energies in addition to the duplication of physical sensations that others feel within in your body. (This might entail feeling the effects of arthritis or something similar when you are near someone who has this affliction— even though you do not suffer from this condition yourself.)

Endocrine glands: Pancreas and spleen. The pancreas governs the balance of sugar in the blood, and it is responsible for utilization by the body in cellular energy production. The spleen has an immune function and is responsible for storing and reabsorbing red blood cells. This relates to how energy is utilized by the body.

Nerve plexus: Solar plexus. This nerve plexus governs the organs of digestion.

Psychological: Related to digestion of information. How we make choices depends upon how we take in information, break it down into component pieces, and then decide what to do with it—store it, use it, or eliminate it.

Color: Yellow. The color relates to mental processes, list making, and analysis.

Keyword: Decision-making. The choices made in living the daily life.

Heart Center (I feel)

Location: Under the center of the breastbone in the middle of the chest.

Governs: Relationship to "Self." Sense of life purpose. Empathy for others.

Psychic function: Emotional plane. Empathy. Understanding the feelings and motives of others.

Endocrine gland: Thymus. Responsible for the T-lymphocytes that are a large part of our immune response.

Nerve plexus: Cardiac. Governs heart and lung function. As we cannot live without oxygen, breathing and heart function go together to pump life force through the physical body, making life possible.

Psychological: Feeling good creates immunity—feeling bad creates vulnerability, not only emotionally, but also physically. Circulation of life force is more than a physical phenomenon. Air carries more than just life-force oxygen, it also carries the solar-electromagnetic charge to the body, which is circulated through the etheric body, making nerve function possible as well as storing vitality. The will to live with a sense of purpose and direction is a spiritual and psychological matter that is translated into physical activity. Feeling compassion for your "self " and others aids decision-making processes.

Color: Green. Nature and nurture. Trust.

Keyword: Connection with true "self." Balance.

Throat Center (I express)

Location: Directly in the throat area.

Governs: Self-expression: speech, conceptual creative activity.

Psychic function: Mental plane. Clairaudience. The ability to hear spirit voices clearly, as if they were speaking in your ear.

Endocrine glands: Thyroid and parathyroid. The thyroid gland is responsible for development of secondary sexual characteristics in maturity. It is also implicated in governing the rate of metabolic processes. The parathyroid glands regulate the amount of available calcium in the blood. Calcium is necessary for strong bones as well as nervous reactivity.

Nerve plexus: Brachial. Governs the arms and neck.

Psychological: Our neck allows us to broaden the scope of our vision, while our arms and hands allow us to manipulate our environment. The ability to reflect upon experiences, make them our own, and to have the courage to communicate them to others is necessary in order for us to mature and to know our "self." This relates to our thyroid function. Metaphorically, parathyroid function relates to creating appropriate structures that lead to appropriate actions. Silent thought or spoken words structure activity.

Color: Turquoise. Freedom of expression, love of language.

Keyword: Self-expression.

Third Eye Center (I have vision)

Location: The brow between the eyes.

Governs: Inner vision. Image-making, imagination.

Psychic function: Mental plane. Clairvoyance is the ability to see clearly. Seeing images, patterns and colors. It also denotes understanding, as in, "I see!"

Endocrine gland: Pituitary. It is the master gland that secretes hormones to control the functions of the rest of the endocrine glands.

Nerve plexus: Sympathetic nervous system. This is responsible for calming down involuntary life functions and also for primitive survival mechanisms—including the emotions.

Psychological: What we can see determines our viewpoints, beliefs, and actions, relating to the function of the pituitary gland. Our ability to see inner color, to access memory via images, and to generate new images or image combinations allows us to have the insights and creative drive that is required for us to manage and manipulate our world.

Color: Indigo blue. Deep thinking, musical, interest in mysteries and psychology.

Keyword: Seeing and understanding.

Crown Center (Me and the planet)

Location: Rises vertically from the center of the brain upward to a height of about five inches.

Governs: Sleeping and waking cycles. Our relationship to available sunlight, our relationship to earth's magnetic north. Shows patterns for potential manifestations in the future.

Psychic function: Spiritual plane. Intuition. The ability to perceive the truth or facts without reasoning.

Endocrine gland: Pineal. Located in the center of the brain beneath the corpus callosum, between the right and left brain hemispheres.

Nerve plexus: Sympathetic nervous system. Responsible for calming down involuntary life functions and primitive survival mechanisms–including the emotions.

Psychological: This is the only vertical chakra, and therefore it connects us to the planet and the stars. Our ability to navigate and to be responsive to the subtleties of planetary existence is condensed within this center. It also holds psychic information about what is to come in to our lives based on what has been seeded in our thought forms.

Color: Violet. Power over heaven and earth. Otherworldly existence.

Keyword: The future. Relationship to the world.

The proper functioning of these centers and the connections between them is vital to our ability to live and function effectively within the world. The process of spiritual self-development affects these chakra centers, clearing them of blockages and gradually bringing them to an ever-higher state of functioning.

3

What Psychics Do

Getting the Message

What psychic readers strive to do (whatever technique they use) is to attune themselves to the client, so that they set up a sympathetic vibration at as many levels as appropriate. Then they feed back to the client what they perceive in a compassionate and sensitive way.

Every psychic uses different tools to retrieve information from the inner planes. Depending on the individual psychic's abilities, he harnesses the understanding of how information is stored and processed on the subtle levels as thought forms, emotions, and sensations. Each psychic uses the tools that he is most comfortable with in order to access information.

Time and time again, my own experience of using different psychic tools has shown me that the techniques and tools may be different but that the messages are very similar. All information is filtered through the energy field and databank of the individual reader.

Psychics act as mirrors to their clients, and they empower clients to take a different viewpoint on decisions and on how these might affect their lives. By reading the patterns of the past, the client can reflect on his choices. By learning in advance the probable patterns of the future, a client can be more optimistic and can feel that he has more personal control over his decision-making. It is often a reframing exercise, whereby the client is shown a different perspective on the things that have been concerning him.

Put like that, it all sounds quite straightforward and easy, doesn't it? Of course it isn't, particularly when one is just starting out on the path of psychic development. Even professionals appreciate the validation they get from clients who call up later to tell them that they were right!

In my work as a teacher of psychic development, there is one question that always comes up and is asked by practically every student. The question is, "*Is it real or just my imagination?*"

Think back to the examples we looked at in the first chapter. How many of these have happened to you? Were they "real" or not, i.e. did they actually happen? The dictionary definition of real is, "existing as a fact, not made up, true, genuine, pertaining to things." So—did you experience it or not? Were the sensations, voices, thoughts, and feelings "real" when they later proved to be genuine, factual, physical manifestations? Yes, of course they were!

This is an understandable question and it is one that will keep cropping up, even when you have learned to trust your inner perception a good deal more than you do now. A large part of the problem is that we are trained only to accept as valid what we can perceive with our physical senses. For example; anyone who "sees" things that others do not will be regarded as being overly imaginative, and things of the imagination are regarded as "unreal."

The hardest thing to do is to learn to be attentive to your perceptions, to trust your inner life, and then have the courage to act upon your perceptions. This can only begin to be reliable by noticing what is real. Our imagination is actually our greatest asset as well as being a liability. Most psychic work takes place within the astral realms, and it is here that our imaginative abilities can create the images that are the "forms" of that world. It is easy to fool yourself, to misinterpret, to make things up, and of course, at the end, to be disappointed and "disillusioned." This is one reason why many religions are negative about psychic work, because there is always the possibility of delusion taking place. That is an important part of what psychic training is about—learning how to access information and to check its validity.

Psychic training teaches us to use the ability to draw on our astral databank in a more reliable way and to use it as a positive creative resource. Expressing your perceptions through words or pictures helps you to evaluate their truth, to make them real and to build confidence.

When I first met my husband, he had difficulty knowing what colors were in someone's aura, because he does not see them. After working with me over the years and seeing the aura drawings that I do, he is now able to identify auric colors, not because he now sees them, but because he intuits or "knows" how to mentally identify them. The information is the same but the manner in which we receive it is different. Either way one has to learn to trust one's perceptions.

Imagination
Your imagination is a special place where decision-making and creative activity take place, either at conscious or subconscious (such as in dreaming) levels. Here is one way of understanding the nature of imagination:

IMAGE—   inner picture gathered and stored from external sensory experience
IN—   within
NATION—   united under the same government = YOU!

It is said that what we can imagine and truly believe in we can make happen, and there is a good deal of truth in that. In the physical world we use our hands and all kinds of tools in order to create things, but in the astral world it is the mind and the power of our imagination that is creative. This is why we have to take care not to impose our own "stuff" when doing psychic readings.

Thought Forms

Thought forms are images that are linked with a thought and with all the other sensory information of the moment, which will become stored within you for further reference. Thought forms are the key to unlocking and working within your inner world, in that they take you back, in every sense, to a moment in the past. These memories provide the foundation for new insights, new decisions, and for creative acts in your life.

Stored thought forms are reperceived within the mind's eye as colored geometric patterns, still pictures, moving pictures, or as barely perceived impressions that flash across a screen. This is something that happens moment-by-moment to us throughout our lives and is an instrumental part of how we process information. It is part of our psychic "self," and it needs to be understood in order to help us come to terms with the amount of information that is at our disposal.

Thought Forms and Sound

We have talked about thought forms as images, but you cannot separate the forms that relate to silent or expressed sound. All sound produces waves that have a shape. This has been demonstrated in experimental conditions by running a bow across a plate containing iron filings. Each vibration (note) produces a unique and consistent pattern of filings to be distributed across the plate. It can also been duplicated by playing a wind or string instrument close to a smoking candle causing each note to produce a unique and consistent spiral pattern in the smoke.

Music generates thought forms. Because I can see energy as color, when I go to a concert I see a "light show" produced by the performance in the area above the musicians. Musical notation is described in terms of color, the chromatic scale being the basis for Western musical expression. *Chromos* is the Greek word for color. Mary Besant, an English clairvoyant working at the beginning of the twentieth century with Reverend Leadbeater, also documented her experiences in seeing colors above orchestras. We are moved by music through the physical beat and the colors and shapes that result from the vibrations produced. These vibrations are perceived and absorbed by us, even when we are not conscious of that fact.

Try this: Prepare to play recordings of several different styles in classical or contemporary music. For example, choose pieces that are peaceful, upbeat, heavy, or dissonant. You may wish to take some notes while you go along, so have a pen and paper handy.

Settle yourself comfortably, relax, close your eyes, and breathe comfortably in silence for a little bit. Then notice how you are within yourself, physically, emotionally, visually, and mentally.

Put on the first piece of music, go back to your
comfortable position, and listen with your eyes
closed. After a while, pay attention to any
feelings that you may experience physically,
emotionally, visually, and mentally. Jot down
your findings.

Repeat through the different musical styles.

Look at your notes and think about how the different
types of music have affected you.

You can also think about how you could use music to
help you in your life. Many psychics and healers use
certain kinds of music to help create a calm, peaceful
environment within which to work, or to move energy in
particular therapeutic ways.

Watch What You Think and Say!

There have been many books written about positive
thinking. Similarly, all religions recommend you to
watch what you think, to refrain from using "bad"
language or gossip, and never to think in anger or to
curse others. Why? Because you are creating and then
sending out powerful negative thought forms! They are
strong cohesive bundles of psychic energy that have a
colored shape. These are heavily loaded with emotions
that have been created within your energy field. They fly
toward the object of your venom and are absorbed by it,
whether the recipient is aware of it or not. Prayer and
distant healing are types of positive thought forms.
Powerful emotions and vivid imagery, combined with
words of intent will be absorbed by the recipient's energy
body or sent to higher powers. Of course, it is not always
other people that are the object of our negative thinking,
because it can also be directed toward us! Worry, guilt,
self-condemnation, and so on, all create negative thought
forms that target us, thereby setting up negative energy

patterns within our own subtle energy fields. Being responsible about what and how you think and what you create is important for everyone, but this is especially so if you are going to develop your psychic abilities. Why? As you become more consciously connected to (and active within) the astral realm, the dominance of your thoughts will magnify and their ability to manifest in reality at a distance will be enhanced.

What Are Messages?

Messages are any kind of communication that is sent from one person to another, or even between different levels of yourself; for instance from your "higher self " to your "lower self ," or from your subconscious to your conscious mind. Some messages arrive unannounced and out of the blue. We can also ask for messages. By posing inner questions, we create a pathway that draws the answer to us, either from some area of our intelligence that we are not normally in touch with, or from other beings such as spirits or inner guides. Exactly how we receive these messages depends on our own psychic structure and strengths. We know that energy vibrations manifest downward from thought, to image, emotions and then to sensations. Messages can be picked up from any of these vibrational "mailboxes." All messages are more easily obtained when you are in a relaxed state.

Mental messages can arrive in many different ways. Frequently they come as answers to inner questions of the "I can hear in it my mind" variety. Alternatively, they can drop in from out of the blue during the course of doing something else, usually something repetitive like washing the dishes. I sometimes find them coming out of my mouth in the course of conversation. I hear words that I did not plan to say—and they sound good! When this happens, I find myself thinking, "Where did that come from?"

Image messages can appear unbidden on the screen before your mind's eye. They can come in dreams or in guided imagery meditations. If you are a visual person, you can use an image to set off a chain of images that will impart information to you. If you can see energy, you will see thought forms and colors or images around people. Once I saw a picture of an ocean liner moving out to sea so clearly in a client's aura that I was shocked. I told her what I saw and she laughed. She told me she had wanted to go on a cruise for about fifteen years and that she had been saving up for it for the past three years. Her thought form was so strong that it had imprinted itself in her aura.

Feeling messages are bursts of emotions or physical sensations. When you step into a room and pick up the emotional atmosphere, this is a type of *feeling* message. Handshakes convey a lot of messages of both feeling types–such as an emotional charge as well as many subtle physical signals. If you are particularly clairsentient, then you may feel another person's physical symptoms. When giving readings, I often find myself having a different taste in my mouth or aches and pains or stiffness that relate to the client rather than to me. *Sensing* earth energies, animals, plants, crystals, and so on can also constitute feeling messages. This is because we are part of the planet, so we have the capacity to attune ourselves to life forces that are sentient and nonsentient.

Signs, portents, and coincidences. These are related to pattern recognition and they arise when repeats of certain events can be linked to together. Their meanings are related yet slightly different. *Signs and portents* are significant warnings or repetitions of pattern. They often come in groups of three, and they appear to happen independently from each other. Although this can be viewed as superstitious, I have found them worth paying attention to, as the repetition of the event often relates to a decision that I need to make, and it can help me make the right one. These omens are also not necessarily related to something evil or negative, because I have discovered that if I follow the message, the outcome will be significantly smoother and easier.

For example, one day I was searching for a new school for my young son. I identified several schools in my area and I sent away for literature on them. Several days later I was chatting with someone who mentioned one particular school that I had not really heard of or considered. I then kept meeting people who independently mentioned that one particular school out of the blue. While out shopping I met someone who mentioned in passing that her children went there and how difficult it had been for them to get in to the school. A pattern was clearly developing, and it was pointing me in the direction of this school. We made an appointment at the school and our son was admitted. The whole process turned out to be smooth, easy, and quick.

Coincidences are the chance occurrence of two things happening at the same time so that they appear to be remarkable or fitting. This is the act or fact of occupying the same time or place.

For example, I was recently visiting my mother and I asked her about someone who lived locally and whom I had known since childhood. My mother responded that this person had not been in touch for about a year and that she did not know what she was doing. My mother and I went our separate ways for the day, but later— when I walked into the flat where I was staying—the phone rang. It was mother, who told me that the phone had been ringing as she walked into her home, and to her surprise, the caller was the very person about whom we had spoken earlier. What a coincidence! What was even better was that this lady said, "I had been sitting at home, thought of you and felt strongly that it was a good moment to call." She then said, "I always pay attention to my strong feelings because experience has shown me that if I follow up on them, they always mean something important."

Interpreting Messages—Are They Literal or Symbolic?

All messages have a basis in a reality that needs to be respected, even if they are sometimes difficult to understand. Interpretation is a skill and an art that depends on building upon your experiences. Remember all the different levels at which we receive messages and apply these simple rules to see how to begin to approach interpreting or understanding the message.

Literal messages are usually straightforward and related to the obvious (to yourself or another). They also relate to real time things and chronology.
Symbolic messages are complex, nonchronological, and seem to appear out of context.

Sometimes, when giving a reading, I do not understand the message, the image, or the feeling.

However, upon sharing it with my client, I find that he understands perfectly what I am talking about. Dreams are a great example of the confusion concerning the need to take a literal or symbolic approach to interpretation. Simply speaking, if the dream is an absurd combination of elements from your past, present, and unknown, then it needs to be interpreted symbolically. If it is a fragment that seems "real" and takes place in "real time" then it needs to be looked at literally.

Refer to later chapters of this book, as they will provide exercises that will help you begin to develop confidence in your ability to interpret what you perceive.

What Do I Do With the Information?
Once information has been received, we have various options. We can express it directly within the context of current conversation—for example, as in a reading. We can hold on to it until a more appropriate moment for expressing it arises, or we can save it for future consideration or reference, either just by remembering it, or (better still) by writing it down. Naturally, we can also discard it as useless. It is important to keep this in mind and to be appropriate in how you use information. You must also be sensitive to the person whom the message is about or the situation that you find yourself in.

How Do I Know How I Am Likely to Receive Information?
We can all get information in many ways, depending upon the type of receiver you happen to be.

The following illustration indicates various types of people according to the chakra system.

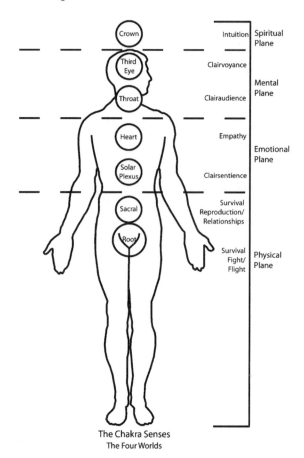

The Chakra Senses
The Four Worlds

CHAKRA	METHOD	HOW IT MANIFESTS
Crown	Intuition	I know
Third eye	Clairvoyance	I see, I think
Throat	Clairaudience	I hear
Heart	Empathy	I feel (emotion)
Solar Plexus	Clairsentience	I feel (sensation)

Here is a test to decide which type of person you are.
Have you ever purchased an item that requires you to
assemble it yourself? Which of the following is your
approach to assembling it:

A: You take only a cursory look at the instructions,
because you prefer to get immersed in the
project, figuring out how it goes together as you
proceed.

B: You look at the pictures to get the feeling of how
it is all supposed to go together, and then maybe
read the instructions briefly.

C: You read the instructions twice to make sure you
understand them, sorting out the pieces as you go
along, so that once you start you know exactly
what you have to do.

D: You take a quick look through the instructions
and all the bits and pieces to get your bearings
and it all seems perfectly clear to you—so away
you go.

Type A indicates that you are an active person who likes
to get things done. You relate more to the
sensation plane. What you feel physically is
important to you. You have "gut feelings" and are
sensitive to the energy of places. You may feel the
physical condition of another person or of an
animal within yourself. You are dominantly
clairsentient and you operate a great deal from
the sacral and solar plexus chakras.

Type B suggests you are an emotional person who
relates to the emotional content of people and
situations. You can tend to become overinvolved
with people or to be hypersensitive to the moods
of others. You may find crowds difficult because
you can be influenced by the dominant emotional

mood, then you find it hard to know which feeling is yours or which belongs to someone else. You are dominantly empathic and you operate from your heart chakra.

Type C denotes that you are a logical sort of person. You think things through and analyze information before speaking. You may or may not have lots of images (*"I see..."*) but you certainly have lots of thoughts! You operate from the mental plane, dominantly from the solar plexus and third eye chakras.

Type D signifies that you tend to be intuitive and that you receive information by means of a mental impression, which then becomes an image and then an emotion and then a sensation. You perceive a pattern and dominantly process information through your crown chakra.

Of course, you can have more than one sense that is strong. I happen to "see" (clairvoyance) and "feel" (empathize) and "sense" (clairsentience) as well as "know" (intuition)—I am not as proficient with clairaudience as with other methods, but I have learned how to operate at that level. You can learn to tap into and use each frequency band. My students and clients often say, "Ooh—I wish I could see the aura like you do." I say that they should focus on doing what comes naturally to them and worry about seeing auras later.

Regardless of the mode that dominates the way that you receive information, the information is exactly the same, *it is just received in a different way!* Despite what some people may try to tell you, no one way is better than any other.

4

You Too Can Develop

The Short Hard Road

Every life is a spiritual challenge, whether the person commits to personal development work or not. People who make that personal commitment take the short hard road. In other words they meet their life challenges willingly, and in the process they accelerate their growth potential. This means becoming aware of strengths in order to overcome weaknesses, facing fears and difficulties with the awareness that there is growth potential inherent in difficulties. The rewards are in *this* lifetime. This offers the potential for using your talents and abilities to empower and help yourself and others, and to be more in touch with nature and the planet. Being true to yourself and your life-purpose brings joy and a sense of rhythm and drive into your life.

"How did *you* develop?" is a question I am often asked. It is always a good question to ask any practicing psychic, because their tale is assured to be an interesting one! Most psychics do not start out wanting to be professional. They end up there after a convoluted journey involving troubles, disappointments, and hardships that are associated with coming to terms with their sensitivities as well as coming to terms with other people. Like any artistic, creative, athletic, or academic achievement, it usually boils down to talent added to hard work over a long period of time! Do not expect to take one or two courses or just read books and bingo, you will be a reliable psychic! It takes work, soul-searching, and a reality check.

Anyone starting now has a terrific advantage, in that psychic training is now more sophisticated and structured in its approach than ever before. This is because it has been more out-in-the-open in the past twenty years. When I reflect upon my own journey, I had to read innumerable books that had been written in the nineteenth and early twentieth centuries to learn about auras and so on. The language was archaic and the information was often inaccurate. There were no psychic courses, just development circles where people were hard-pressed or reluctant to answer questions because they thought it was not "spiritual" to do anything other than blindly accept what was being said without question.

I had to study divination techniques, psychology, spiritual philosophies of Eastern and Western religions, and meditation—all separately. I subsequently put all that information and experience together into a training package that made sense in modern times—and in modern language designed to meet modern needs. I have since discovered that many gifted psychics and healers born in the mid–twentieth century were coincidentally drawn to do the same thing.

Some Inspirational Stories

Below are some condensed tales regarding the development of some extraordinary readers I have met. The common thread here is that each person was drawn to (or pushed by) life circumstances to pursue their development path from within as a matter of spiritual conviction, and this was conjoined with certain outer experiences that influenced them. They also had to operate outside of conventional society's expectations for a while in order to develop and come to terms with their gifts. I have changed all the names for the sake of anonymity.

Professor of Economics to Astrologer, Card Reader, and Clairvoyant

Gordana was a professor of economics at the University of Sarajevo. She always had an interest in spiritual matters and started reading every available book on astrology, then doing charts for friends and family–although her life was more involved with academic frameworks, teaching, and her family life. From a part-time passion, astrology became her second job, and just a few months before the outbreak of war, she opened an astrological company.

With the outbreak of war in the former Yugoslavia, she had to abandon her life there and flee to the UK with her children, and start a new life as a refugee. She had to learn a new language and find a new career path. During this transitional time, Gordana also took development courses, studying Tarot and clairvoyance in London. She attained her diplomas and subsequently chose to become a professional reader with the British Astrological and Psychic Society.

Music Management Consultant to Clairvoyant and Card Reader

Nicole began working in her teens in music and nightclub management and she then ran her own music production company and recording studio. She also managed artists and provided contracts for numerous musical production companies. On occasions when she had a bit too much to drink, she was told that she channeled information without being aware of how this was happening. Much to her amazement, this information usually proved to be true. By coincidence, Nicole then met a psychic lady who introduced her to many different spiritual traditions. This lady also taught Nicole basic card-reading skills. Nicole began to open up her own psychic abilities. She began giving card readings to friends and she also took development classes. Nicole changed many things in her life during this time, as she decided to go back to school and study counseling in addition to training as a crystal healer. Nicole changed jobs and began to work in human resources management, where she quietly used many of her new skills.

Her abilities blossomed, came under more conscious control, and expanded beyond card reading to reliable clairvoyance and mediumship. She now works as a psychological counselor, making use of her psychic skills in addition to giving readings.

Language Teacher to Clairvoyant Tarot Card Reader

While working as a teacher of French and Spanish, Karen felt drawn to begin reading every book on spiritual philosophy that she could get her hands on. This lead Karen to practice meditation, and she eventually moved into an ashram for a period of intense spiritual practice. One day, she was shocked to see a brilliant blue light around someone–then the light promptly disappeared. Intense tingling in her third eye area disturbed her sleep, and for a while she thought something was wrong with her. A friend from the ashram explained that her inner sight was opening. This friend recommended a Silva Mental Dynamics course, which provided Karen with a practical format for her growing clairvoyance. At first, she was reluctant, but then a next-door neighbor who was moving away rang her bell and handed her a pack of Tarot cards, saying that she thought Karen might like them. She started playing around with them and another friend taught her some of the basics.

Karen then started to ask inner questions and to use the cards to get answers, and she had a lot of fun giving readings to herself and to others. She continued to carry on with her meditation work all the while. After having her son, her psychic faculties opened up even more. Karen gave up teaching but she still did not want to do professional psychic work. After a series of difficult personal experiences, Karen was forced to think about making a living. She chose to teach development courses and to give readings in a focused way, promoting and taking responsibility for her own gifts in the world. Every time she tried to do something other than readings with her life it did not work out, and each time someone would come to her for psychic advice, so she could not avoid working in the psychic field.

Ways to Develop

Start with what interests you and what you know about. Begin to notice things more, to ask basic questions about who you are, where you are going, why you are here, what you are good and not so good at, and what keeps repeating in your life. Read lots of books, take classes, and examine what is happening in your life rather than what you would like to happen. Look at your life.

There is a saying among psychics that when the student is ready, the teacher appears. This saying is so true! We attract to us the things that we need—even if we do not think that we need it! Many people who enter our lives can be potential teachers, so we need to find a few role models to emulate along our personal journey. Some can answer questions and others will pose more questions for us to think about!

Working with groups is also useful; this way you discover that others have had similar experiences, and you all have a context for sharing. More people equals more energy and more inspiration. Choose your teacher with care. You become the teacher's "child" for a while —and children learn by copying their parents. Let the saying "By their fruits ye shall know them" be your guide. Observe the teacher's life and see what he or she has created, but do not put them on a pedestal. Appreciate all their qualities in perspective. Relate what you are learning to every aspect of your life. Eventually you will have to leave the teacher and the group in order to step out on your own and to make that knowledge your own.

Responsibility

Definition: Obliged or expected to account for, involving obligation or duties, trustworthy, reliable.

When you begin your journey in earnest, you will start to take responsibility for your actions. Greater knowledge brings greater responsibility. You can no longer blame others for your problems. Realize that each action that you take has consequences. Appreciate that you bear joint responsibility within relationships. Realize that you can only control yourself, not others. Understand that others can only control you when you give them the means to do so. Responsibility brings peacefulness rather than just duty, because there is an understanding about what is yours. You can be more aligned in your attitudes and therefore less conflicted.

Relationships

Your relationships can change a lot when you begin your inner work. This is because you are changing your viewpoint and redefining yourself. It is a fact that being true to yourself means being aligned to your personal and moral and ethical life. It can mean standing up for yourself or striving to change negative behavior patterns.

It means letting go of worn-out relationships and, being less sociable, because you may need to spend more time alone for a while. People may tell you that you have changed. Well, expect that, and accept that change is a good thing—though it can be difficult to travel down the road when there are no signposts!

Spiritual Development

You cannot separate your psychic development from your spiritual development. Remember that contained within the definition of *psychic* is soul, and that your psychic world reflects your soul's manifestation in the world. Your outlook, beliefs, and habits are also a reflection of this. Spiritual development means asking deep questions about your beliefs and how you live them on a daily basis.

"Spiritual" does not necessarily mean religious. Religions are systems of faith and worship of a Supreme Being. They therefore offer a particular pathway to knowledge of God within. You can have faith in the order of the universe and a creator, and still choose not to belong to a religion. In fact, it is extremely useful to look at different religious beliefs, because they all explain the same phenomena of creation and life, in different ways. This type of study often brings you into a deeper relationship with the religion that you were taught as a child. There are more similarities between the various religions than religious leaders may acknowledge. The paths are many, but the truth is one! The problems come from people's interpretation of spiritual law, added to the political power aspects of religious belief. Once people are caught up in that, they often forget the deeper messages of oneness, harmony, and peace within the self and toward others that God consciousness is purported to bring.

You can reach God consciousness by washing dishes! It is not *what* you do, but *how* you do it that counts in development work. Effective psychic training teaches you that your psychic life *is* your life. It encompasses all that you are and all that you do. It is imperative to relate what you learn to what is happening in your life, within you and outside of you. Your spiritual life is *all* of your life!

Change

Definition: Change means to make or become different, to alter, transmute, or transform.

Be prepared–it may not be what you expect! You may seek to develop yourself because there are elements in your life that you are dissatisfied with, or potential that is unrealized. These are great motivators. When we change one element of our lives, the rest of the picture is also changed. Sometimes we forget this, and we are surprised by the repercussions of our thought, word, or deed.

The Chinese say that the only thing that is constant is *change*. This is not a standard Western assumption. We seek balance, stability, and consistency. However, these concepts frequently do not imply change, but immovability and permanence. In psychic development work, we redefine these terms.

Balance is a dynamic state, not a static one. Appropriateness is the defining criterion.

Stability is about your relationship with yourself. The ability to consult your center and to have confidence in the way you make decisions and back them up.

Consistency is more about your approach to things, and being true to yourself.

The nature of change and growth is cyclic. We are part of nature, so we can learn a great deal about the patterns of birth, growth, maturity, old age, and death by examining these cycles. Each of our bodies has its own cyclic rhythm. When they are harmonious with one another, we are more at peace with our self.

How much are you willing to push the boundaries, to move beyond your present comfort zone? This will determine the rate and depth of your development.

Obstacles

Some of the difficulties that I see people encountering in their psychic studies is that they want to fly too high too fast. They cannot wait to see the aura, contact the spirits, use their "powers" etc. Without proper roots, the tree blows over in the first big storm. Develop the roots, and the tree grows tall, the crown spreads wide.

It is important to understand that development takes time. We can only change slowly, by seeing ourselves and what we do, by trying new approaches to problem solving, and by repetition of new behaviors. These are life lessons that we can repeat throughout our lives–because this is how long it often takes to change our karmic patterns in awareness!

The greatest obstacles to change and growth are negative attitudes. Why? Because they are really deeply embedded thought forms! You can never totally rid yourself of them, as they are stored in your astral databank, but you can replace them with stronger, positive thought forms. Here are some of the most frequent negative thoughts to look out for:

Blaming someone else for something you may need to take some responsibility for.
Resistance means acting against or opposing something. Sometimes this attitude is appropriate, but it also

can be a signal of avoidance. Moving through this attitude to a task or outlook is very rewarding and helps build confidence.

A negative attitude is telling yourself how stupid, bad, useless etc. you are. How often are you your own worst judge? How often does this critical behavior produce positive results, or does it just make you feel worse?

Fear means making bad movies in your head. Fear generates worst-case scenarios that get blown out of proportion and may have nothing to do with what is actually happening!

Comparing yourself to others can be an unrewarding obstacle. We can learn from others and it is important to appreciate what they have to offer, however, no matter how we see them, it is hard to appreciate that they have their own issues and difficulties. How about concentrating on your own achievements and abilities?

Mystery and illusion. Some people turn to psychic work in order for others to see them as mysterious, glamorous, or powerful. Powerful people make things happen. Become truly powerful in yourself, and you can make things happen to empower others, not to "wow" people or frighten them. Life is a great mystery. The need to impress others points to insecurity rather than confidence. Truly confident people are "being here now." What kind of impression do you want to make?

The more you work on positive skills by looking at what is and dealing with that, and by using your sensitivity to understand yourself and others, the more you will gain from your development work. Start at the bottom and work your way up. This means learning to use psychic principles practically in real life situations. Then you will have the skills to go on to higher contacts and states of consciousness.

5

Keeping Track

Contact with your inner world is the beginning of getting to know yourself better. It is surprising how easy it is to forget where you started from, so a development record will provide you with a clear view of your pathway.

Make a journal and record your progress. Buy a binder to which you can add and subtract pages, or dedicate a file on your computer. This way you can go back and see where you have come from, and that will help you see where you are going!

Writing things down will help you to ground them and to make your experiences more real. This helps you not only to validate your perceptions and experiences but also to help put them into perspective. Be creative in your journal by drawing pictures. This form of grounding helps unclutter your brain, allowing you to see patterns where formerly there were only jumble and confusion.

An understanding of your own patterns is an important foundation in being able to discern what is *you* and what is *the other*. It helps you to interpret what you receive more easily. The current of habitual ways of thinking and feeling carves deep thought-form channels into the riverbank of the subconscious mind. Using our awareness of the structure of how we process inner information and our thought-forms puts us in touch with new possibilities of perception, belief, and behavior.

In learning to navigate the astral plane, you will begin to recognize the repeating patterns of your inner world.

Cultivating Your Inner Observer

Observing implies taking note of what is happening without judging or analyzing. Cultivating an inner observer is the key to developing a greater ability to perceive clearly and sharply.

Imagine a little video camera inside your head that is recording what you are seeing. You can do this with your eyes open as well as with your eyes closed. You can run the videotape back and observe what happened, and *then* begin to make sense of it.

Until you begin to have some distance from the habits of reaction you cannot begin to know how to act by making conscious choices and decisions. You also block out information that may be useful to you.

Recording a Positive Journal

The object of this is to train your inner observer to develop a different perspective over life events, to begin to perceive patterns, to become more attentive to language, and to reframe the way you think in a more positive manner. Remember that you are choosing what to write, and that constitutes thought forms. We have been taught that to be critical is to be negative, so what we wish to promote here is positive thinking. Sometimes people think that positive thinking is overly optimistic and "nice." Positive thinking stimulates creativity, energy, and confidence. Your subconscious mind relates words to emotional reality. Learning to reframe your outlook will change how you see the world. It will also show you how negative others' self-esteem is by their use of language.

Keep a small notebook and pen by your bedside, and every evening before going to sleep, write down any important events and insights that you have experienced. Think before you write. *You are only allowed to express yourself using positive language.* Even if what happened to you was upsetting or difficult, find a positive way to say it.

Negative example: I failed the test today. I am totally discouraged because I will never be able to learn it and pass.

Positive example: I failed the test today. Now I know what areas I need to revise in order to achieve success the next time that I take it.

Recording Meditations and Exercises

Have you ever awakened from a vivid dream and later find that you cannot recall it at all? The higher your psychic work goes, the more difficult it is to bring the information back. It is therefore important to record any experiences that you have in your meditations or in the exercises that you do. This is also a form of grounding, as it trains you to bridge the gap between your inner and outer states of awareness. This overcomes the problems that you will meet when trying to retain the things that you experience on the inner levels.

6

The Nature of Time

The way we have been conditioned to perceive time is based upon the cycles of the physical world. That is the day (the sun), the week (the moon's quarters), the month (the moon), and the year (the Earth's movement around the sun). This also governs how we define the past, present, and future.

When you are really bored, time creeps—you keep looking at your watch and a minute seems like an hour. Conversely, as the saying goes, "Time flies when you are having fun!" I have found this is really true. Perception of time has to do with our emotions and how engaged we are in the moment. When we are impatient, time seems to slow down and we get frustrated, but at other times it rushes past us.

Time on the physical plane is different from time in the astral or nonphysical world. Time in the astral plane is like the time that you experience in the dream world. Instead of being governed by physical forces, it is governed by thought forms. In your imagination, you can travel to any part of the world immediately rather than being held up by the constraints of travel in the physical world. Your dream dramas can seem like they are epic in length, yet they actually take place over a few minutes. If you are engrossed in a meditation, it is often for much longer than you expected. If you are in a daydream, time stops. In fact, the phrase "time out" expresses a state where one steps out of the perceived constraints of the physical plane in order to "come back to yourself." The worlds of the mind and imagination have different measures of time, and this phenomenon is often emotional in nature. Timing on the inner planes can often be inaccurate, which is why future predictions can be hard to pinpoint as far as timing is concerned.

For example: I once had a premonition that there would be some problems in a country that I was scheduled to travel to. I saw civil unrest and difficulties but could not "see" the exact cause. I decided to cancel my trip, much to the dismay of others involved. Several days after I had been scheduled to arrive there, an earthquake destroyed much of the roadways and disrupted service infrastructures. I was glad to have cancelled the trip. My perception was proven to be accurate, but the timing was slightly off. In addition, the civil unrest I had seen was not due to rioting, but to disruption of life due to the disaster.

The subconscious mind exists in perpetual present-time reality. This is why it is so difficult to interpret premonitions, psychic experiences, and some dreams.

7

Foundation Skills

I cannot emphasize strongly enough the importance of sound foundation skills for any psychic work. Whether this concerns meditation, reading, or healing, the situation is the same. Just as you have to learn how to cross the street safely (stop, listen, and look both ways, and then walk) so you also need to learn safe steps that will enable you to navigate the inner realms.

It is also surprising that many of the problems that people encounter in every day life are also profoundly addressed by learning these foundation skills. These are *boundary* issues; *space* issues, *control* issues, and *safety* issues.

I recommend that you work through them one by one in order, and pay particular attention to the Breathing and Cosmic Cross exercises, because these provide the foundation for the rest of the work.

Elements of Energy Control

Energy Control is the ability to regulate, limit, or direct the manifestation of energy through intention (intention = deciding to make it happen). This is a primary principle of energy transformation, or bringing subtle energies down into manifestation. Another word for this is the act of *creation*. We began to explore some of these ideas in previous chapters. Although this sounds very high-flown and very profound, it happens every moment of our lives! Every idea, notion, or thought we allow into our minds has creative potential, and the more emotional energy we inject into it, the more that thought manifests into action by creating either an object or an event.

Coming into a greater sense of control over your inner state begins with understanding the principles of how all creation happens and the cycle of energy flow from the spiritual to the physical world, through thought, word, and deed.

Our actions then influence our feelings and our thoughts, which begins the cycle once again. The sum of our life experiences is then reintegrated into our spiritual dimension.

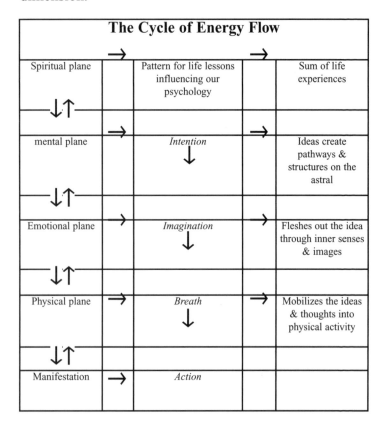

The Cycle of Energy Flow					
	→		→		
Spiritual plane		Pattern for life lessons influencing our psychology		Sum of life experiences	
↓↑	→		→		
mental plane		*Intention* ↓		Ideas create pathways & structures on the astral	
↓↑	→		→		
Emotional plane	→	*Imagination* ↓	→	Fleshes out the idea through inner senses & images	
↓↑					
Physical plane	→	*Breath* ↓	→	Mobilizes the ideas & thoughts into physical activity	
↓↑					
Manifestation	→	*Action*			

We have already looked at the influence and importance of thought forms on the inner levels and the need to mobilize them within the context of psychic work. Now, let us look at breath.

Breath Is Life

Principles of Breathing. It's so simple—right? Wrong. The simplest things are often the hardest to understand and those which bring the most rewards. We start at the simple beginning, which is breathing.

Breath Is Life. We cannot live for more than three minutes without breathing. Breathing is an automatic function that we ignore at our peril. It is also more than just the exchange of oxygen and carbon dioxide. It is the interchange between our internal and external environments, our means of acquiring and circulating life force through our energy system, a direct route into our psychological self. We have said that in order to make anything happen, we apply our intention, imagination, and breath. Breath acts as the link between our inner life and our ability to manifest it outward.

The Hindus developed an in-depth methodical approach called Pranayama—or the science of breath control—into a spiritual art. The name is a combination of Sanskrit words. *Prana* means "life force" and *yama* means "control." The study and practice of Pranayama brings the practitioner to different states of consciousness through methodical manipulation of the phases within the cycle of breathing and control over breathing physiology. This ancient art has much to teach us at every level of psychic work. It is so simple, yet its results are so profound.

The prime saying in Pranayama teaching is, *"Breath follows mind as mind follows breath."* In other words, our state of mind affects our breathing as our breathing affects our state of mind.

For example, if we are anxious, our breathing pattern is irregular, shallow, and rapid. When we are calm, our breathing pattern is regular, deep, and slow. We can therefore calm our anxiety by consciously slowing, deepening, and regularizing our pattern of breathing. Regular rhythm creates order and stability of thought.

We can understand this by looking at the cycle of breath in three dimensions: rhythm, depth, and duration.

Rhythm: Regular or irregular pattern of breathing.
Depth: How deeply the air descends into the lungs or which part of the lungs are most active in the physical process of breathing.
Duration: How rapidly or slowly each phase within a breathing cycle is done.

Anatomy of Breathing

We can consciously manipulate the breath by understanding the physical cycle of breathing. Inhalation is an automatic process, triggered either by the level of carbon dioxide in the blood or by nerve stimulus. Deep exhalation is a voluntary process. People usually do not exhale adequately. They also do not use a great proportion of their lung capacity. Most people are aware of using the front part of their ribs and tummy when breathing rather than their back or complete rib cage. They also breathe more into the top portion of the lungs, rather than deeply into them, forcing the shoulders to tense and rise. This is the body's way of compensating for the decrease in lung capacity. Our goal is therefore to regulate the depth of our breathing. This requires the effort of retraining your breathing technique.

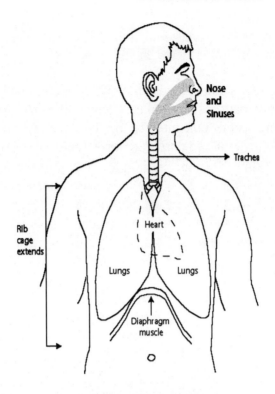

Lungs and Breathing Apparatus

The lungs are large organs, extending from just beneath the collarbone to beneath the lower ribs. The rib cage, though expandable, is considerably more rigid in its upper portion surrounding the chest than in its lower portion around the back and abdominal area. It can be likened to the action of a bellows, opening more below than above as it sucks air into the lungs by opening up and pushes air out by decreasing its size. It does this in conjunction with the diaphragm muscle that sits just beneath the ribs and separates the abdominal cavity from the thoracic (chest) cavity. On inhalation, the diaphragm muscle expands downward and outward in conjunction with the interior intercostal muscles (between the ribs) to expand the rib cage, thereby increasing the volume (capacity) of the lungs, which in turn makes for a greater exchange of gases between the structures of the lungs and blood.

We need to learn how to use all of our lung capacity.

Breathing Exercises

Do all of these exercises and then practice them from time to time. Before beginning, sit comfortably in an upright position, with your eyes closed, your feet flat on the floor, and with hands resting in your lap. Relax physically and observe your breathing—its natural rhythm, depth, and duration. Make a mental note of it for comparison at the end of each of the exercises.

One: Simple Conscious Breathing

The object of this exercise is to consciously prepare yourself and continue to breathe rhythmically, slowly, and deeply. Do this for several minutes. Concentrate on the physical sensations of the breathing process, then revert to natural breathing and observe any changes. You will notice that you will feel very relaxed and more inward when you manage to concentrate on the physical sensation of breathing. This happens even after a very short period of time.

Two: Awareness of the Different Areas of Your Lungs

The purpose of this exercise is for you to become aware of the role of the whole of the lungs when used in the breathing process, as well as the particular areas where you are and are not breathing fully. Imagine the lungs being divided into three sections, which are lower, middle, and upper.

Place your hands firmly on the lower portion of your rib cage below the breastbone and along the side, then breathe in deeply, slowly, and only briefly, until you feel that section expanding. Hold, exhale, then repeat.

Repeat this process by moving your hands up, placing your hands on the ribcage firmly at the level just above the end of the breastbone. Again, try breathing into that portion of the lungs only briefly, until you feel that section expanding, then hold, exhale, and repeat.

Repeat this process by placing the palms of your hands on your chest just below the collarbone. Again, try to isolate the sensation of expansion upon exhalation without involving the rest of the lungs.

Now, connect the breath between the sections. Inhale lower, middle, then upper—hold—exhale lower, middle, and upper—pause. Repeat until you really can feel the filling, exchange, emptying, and neutrality of the lungs working during the breathing cycle.

Now, I can hear you are saying to yourself "What! Exhale lower, middle, upper—impossible!" Believe me, you will get used to it. Although it takes a while to build the new habit, it will become easy, and you will experience benefits. It is important to breathe through your nose, as this is the organ constructed for that purpose. Many people also tense their jaws, shoulders, and abdomen unnecessarily as they breathe, so be aware of this and relax!

Three: Back Breathing Exercise

When breathing, it is important to use the whole rib cage, which includes your back and spine. We are three-dimensional physical beings, and what is behind us is metaphorically and literally significant! It is better to concentrate on breathing into your back. This has psychological implications, as most people do not pay much attention to their back, to what is behind them, or to their difficult relationships with their past. They cut off their awareness of a fundamental portion of their persona and the foundation of what has been that affects them in the present. By mobilizing awareness in your back, you have an opportunity to heal many things in your past without resorting to analytical methods. Just breathe and it all comes up for you to take a look at.

Sit in a comfortable upright position, leaning against pillows that support your back. When you inhale, be aware of your whole rib cage progressively expanding and pressing gently into the pillows. Conversely, when you exhale, be aware of the rib cage contracting. Continue; be aware of the movement of muscles and air throughout the length of the spine and not solely in one area. Observe any changes.

Try this while lying on your back on the floor with your knees raised and arms loosely by your sides, palms facing upwards. As you breathe, feel the movement of your spine pressing against the floor's surface.

Now try it sitting unsupported, and see if you can feel a more three-dimensional breathing action.

Duration

Let us now look at the matter of duration. When asked, many people think there are two phases within one cycle of breath, which are in and out. Some notice three phases, which are in, hold, and out. In fact, one cycle of breath has four phases, which are inhale, hold, exhale, and pause. Each phase relates to a particular physical and psychospiritual state. It is useful to liken these states to the four seasons.

Each phase corresponds to the movement of breath, and by changing the duration of each phase you will alter your state of consciousness. Work through the exercises, and eventually you will begin to understand and link these concepts through your experiences.

Inhale: Taking in breath initiates the breathing cycle. You fill your lungs with oxygen and life force through your nose. The act of inhalation kick-starts

PHASE	INHALE	HOLD	EXHALE	PAUSE
State	Outer	Inner	Outer	Inner
Correspondence	Spring	Summer	Autumn	Winter
Correspondence	Initiating	Consolidating	Releasing	Stillness
Correspondence	East	South	West	North

certain physiological reactions. It brings a smile to the corners of your mouth, which stimulates endorphins to be released into your brain, making you happy; the air passing through the sinuses stimulates the hypothalamus gland that governs the rest of your endocrine system. The air is warmed and filtered through the nasal passages, so you begin to fill and nourish your life-force and oxygen levels. Spring is a time of new growth, happiness, and hope. It is an initiating energy that stimulates the mind. Inhalation is an outwardly positive act, which is why it is so recognizable.

Hold: When you hold your breath, the body is at the height of the business of exchanging oxygen from the lungs and transmitting it to the arterial blood and shifting the carbon dioxide from the venous blood back into the lungs in preparation for exhalation. In a way this is like the summer, the height of the heat. In fact when you hold your breath, the mind is very active and heat and tingling sensations build up in the body. This phase is internally active.

Exhale: Exhaling expels carbon dioxide and stimulates energy circulation. Like the autumn leaves being blown from a tree by the wind, we must let go of things that are no longer useful to us. It is again an externally active phase of breath and one that often accompanies external activity.

Pause: By the time you reach the pause, you have reached an oxygen-neutral state. In other words, you are fully nourished, and the body is utilizing the oxygen but not yet creating a great deal of carbon dioxide. This is a quiet time inwardly, like winter, still and frozen, the perfect launch pad for meditation.

Now it is time to have some practice in manipulating the duration of each of these phases. As you move through each phase, count in your mind. Focus on the physical breathing process and keep your inner observer switched on. If you find any phase uncomfortable, consciously relax your face, shoulder, and tummy muscles during that phase. Also, identify how it is uncomfortable for you physically, emotionally, or mentally. It is not unusual to find one or more phases more difficult to handle. How might this relate to some of your own inner issues? Make notes. You will find that with practice over time, you will be able to overcome some of the breathing difficulties associated with that particular phase with a concomitant psychological change.

You will also find that the more you breathe in any of these patterns that you naturally begin to count more slowly through each phase. Eventually you can stop counting, yet stay true to the rhythm that you have initiated.

Exercise

Sit in a comfortable upright position and relax. Later you can try this after activating your Cosmic Cross. Mentally put yourself inside a shiny golden eggshell. This will consolidate your energies, as outlined later in the Cosmic Cross Exercise.

Keep your internal observer on and breathe to the counted pattern, as follows:

Inhale 4, Hold 4, Exhale 4, Pause 4. Repeat at least 10 times. Allow your breathing to return to its normal unmanipulated rhythm. Note your observations.

Inhale 4, Hold 2, Exhale 4, Pause 2. Repeat at least 10 times. Allow your breathing to return to its normal unmanipulated rhythm. Note your observations.

Inhale 2, Hold 4, Exhale 2, Pause 4. Repeat at least 10 times. Allow your breathing to return to its normal unmanipulated rhythm. Note your observations.

Conscious breathing is the foundation of all controlled inner work and is something to constantly go back to in your life. This is also a wonderful way of stopping heart palpitations and of calming the mind when one is anxious. It is a great teacher.

Space and Boundaries

Space is the room or place that extends around you. A boundary is a limiting line or border. Both are issues for everyone at some point in their lives. Our perception of how much space we take up, or that we have available to us, relates to how we express our personality in the world. Boundaries are tied up with our sense of self and our limitations, including how we allow others to come into our space and to influence us. People often have clearer boundaries in their working lives where protocols and limitations are already demarcated within their professional roles. In their emotional lives, the boundaries can be a lot less clear. Generally speaking, the more confident you are in yourself, the more established your boundaries are. You "know your limitations" and can choose to take risks and stretch those boundaries or not.

In our look at the shape of the human energy field, we see there are natural boundaries formed by differences in vibrational frequency that influence the structure and function of each level. Our bodies have a natural space and shape or sphere of existence and influence. Since life means change, then changes in the space and shape of each body fluctuate to reflect this.

We need to be able to become more aware of the space and shape of our more dense energy fields in order to begin to obtain a greater sense of cohesiveness and alignment, and a way to go within and come back out more efficiently. Knowing that we can mobilize thought forms to aid us in this task, we can build a flexible and appropriate structure using thought forms into our awareness to help us gain better sense of our boundaries.

Cosmic Cross Exercise

This visualization provides the basis for defining your boundaries and for strengthening and energizing your energy field. It is a means of psychic protection and a useful tool in healing practice. It provides the starting point for all psychic or healing work as well as the basis of cleansing and protection. In other words, it is vital for effective energy management.

The first step is to build the Cosmic Cross into your aura through repeated visualization exercises. The Cosmic Cross should be generated using your intention and imagination, and then mobilized through conscious breathing. Through repetition, you will become distinctly aware of its presence around you. This will be accompanied by a sense of well-being, separateness and balance, which will provide you with a means of centering your psychic energies.

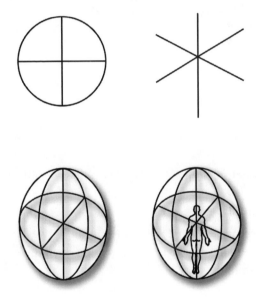

The beauty of the Cosmic Cross is that it represents a naturally occurring energy phenomenon, and therefore you are not building something alien into your energy structures, only enhancing what is already there. By creating a new thought form within your aura you are laying in a wiring system and all that will be required is for you to turn the light switch on to activate the image. Once you are accustomed to activating your Cosmic Cross, it takes only seconds! Eventually, when mentally saying "Cosmic Cross," you turn on the inner light switch at the center of your being and the Cosmic Cross springs into existence as a whole.

Technique
Read the following visualization to yourself several times. Then, dictate it slowly onto an audiotape and do the exercise. The initial visualization process is divided into three sections—establishing the triple cross, establishing the circles, and establishing the bubble. You will then need to practice activating the Cosmic Cross over the course of at least a week, doing it several times a day in order to master this visualization.

The Cross
Sit comfortably upright in your chair and begin to breathe slowly and deeply.

Concentrate your attention on the area between the heart and solar plexus centers. See and feel a ball of white/gold light shining brightly like a sun. Using your breath and imagination, project a line of light from this ball and allow the light to extend vertically through the center of your body. Extend the beam of light upward through the top of the head and downward through the genital area directly into the center of the earth. Breathe, and establish this vertical shaft of light, being aware of the flow of energy in both directions.

Return your attention to the center of light and project
another line to the left and to the right into the
distance, breathing and being aware of energy
flowing through that line activating it. You now
stand within a regular cross.

Return your attention to the center of light and project
another line in front and behind you into the
distance, breathing and being aware of energy
flowing through that line and activating it. You
now stand within a three-dimensional cross that
is suspended in space.

The Circles

Next, mentally draw a circle around you, starting at a
point a foot or so above your head on the vertical
shaft and arcing downward in front of you,
connecting with the front shaft. Allow this to pass
through the ground beneath between your feet,
connecting with the downward shaft; then arcing
upward behind you, connecting with the
backwards shaft, and finally onward until it
reconnects above your head. This describes a
complete circle around you as if you were
standing within a large hoop that goes around
you from front to back.

The second circle is drawn horizontally, commencing at
the intersection of the circle and vertical shaft
above your head, arcing down to the left. This
intersects with the horizontal shaft, continues
down to connect beneath the feet at the junction
of the vertical beam and the first circle, then
curves upward to connect with the right
horizontal line and meets itself back at the top.
Now you have a second hoop that goes around
you from side to side.

The final circle is drawn horizontally like an equator. Inscribe the circle in a clockwise direction, connecting the four horizontal shaft and circle interstices all around, starting and finishing in front of you.

Retract the horizontal lines until they meet the circles, making a sphere shape that surrounds you. You will be contained within an integrated linear basket-like structure that is floating in space.

Establishing the Bubble

Now, visualize an iridescent membrane completely covering the skeleton structure of the circled cross so that you are completely contained in a translucent bubble of energy and light, balanced within yourself with clear boundaries. Inwardly say "I am within my Cosmic Cross, my energy bubble." Take a few moments to observe your state of physical, emotional, and mental being. When you are ready to return to predominantly greater awareness of the outer world, take a deep breath in, raise your arms above your head and stretch. Now, as you lower your arms—open your eyes and exhale. Take a moment to be aware of your state of being.

Activation

Now that you have drawn your Cosmic Cross line by line, it is permanently programmed into your system! All you have to do is "turn on the switch" to activate the Cosmic Cross. You must embed this visualization through repetition and practice, putting it up quickly and in a more condensed fashion. This takes time. If you practice doing this several times a day over the next week you will master this technique in no time and it will change your life.

First, practice activating it by mentally saying "Cosmic Cross" and put up the triple cross, then the circles, then the membrane.

The next few times start by imagining all the lines lighting up from the center, like a sunburst, as you say "Cosmic Cross" and see and/or feel it light up and be established. This is the easiest and fastest way to do it.

Once this visualization is established, we will refer to the finished product as your "Energy Bubble" or "Energy Egg," and once you find this easy to do, you can put it to good use.

Expansion and Contraction Exercise Using the Cosmic Cross

Back to space and boundaries! Now that you know your "energy shape," you can learn to become more aware and you can also learn to manipulate that shape and space.

Read the steps through several times until you can remember what to do, or dictate it slowly onto an audiotape, giving yourself enough time to do each stage of the exercise. I recommend that you *do* the exercise before going to the evaluation explanation. It will then make *real* sense to you.

Beginning the Exercise

Sit down in a comfortable upright position, feet flat on the floor, and hands placed comfortably on your lap. Relax and let go of any physical tension you may have.

Close your eyes and observe your state of being physically, emotionally, and mentally. You will be able to hold this and recall it at the end of your meditation.

Begin to breathe slowly, deeply, and rhythmically and when you are ready, *activate your Cosmic Cross.*

Once you are within your energy bubble, breathe and become more aware of the space around you and the energy that is circulating within and around you.

Now, focus your attention on your center and move your awareness outward until you reach the inner surface of your energy bubble. Feel that you can touch this membrane and follow its inner boundary surface all around you; above you; to the right; downward; to the left; beneath you; and in front of you. Become aware that as you use your inner eyes to look, your attention will heighten your awareness of that area. This is your energy space. This energy space relates to your personality body—your denser astral field.

Take a few moments to breathe and consciously move energy through all of the energy pathways (up, down, and horizontal) in your Cosmic Cross so that the spaces in between become really charged with life force.

Next, you will *expand* your energy space and boundary. Imagine that with every complete breath, your energy space is expanding outward in every direction. The arms of your Cosmic Cross are moving outward in each direction. The membrane is not getting thinner but extending to accommodate the expansion, as if you were blowing up a balloon. Slowly extend your awareness outward in all directions, until you fill the room; then the rooms around that room; out into the street; and then stop. Stay in that expanded state for several minutes and observe your state of being. Tell your subconscious mind to remember.

Draw your attention back in to your center, and prepare to slowly contract your energies. Imagine that with every inhalation you begin to withdraw the length of each ray as well as your outer membrane toward you, contracting the space within your Cosmic Cross progressively. Inhale and draw in. Hold and contract more. Exhale and circulate those energies through your energy body. Pause and absorb. Repeat this until your energy bubble surrounds you to a distance of about two feet.

Stay in that contracted state for several minutes, breathing, relaxing, and circulating your energies. *Observe* your state of being. Tell your subconscious mind to remember.

Take a deep breath in, and instruct your energy field with the next series of breaths to revert to its normal, comfortable space around you. Be aware, as you continue the breathing cycle, of your field expanding outward again to its optimum breadth around you. Keep breathing, and once your energy bubble has reached that state, relax and *observe* your state of being.

Before coming back into "waking" awareness, take a few moments to mentally review and compare the different experiences between the four energy states, that is, before activating your Cosmic Cross, your expanded state, your contracted state, and your "normal" bubble state.

When you are ready to come back, take a deep breath in, raise your arms above your head, and stretch. Lower your arms, exhale, and open your eyes. Write down your experience of the different energy states.

Reflections upon the Exercise

Congratulations! You have just manipulated the shape and space within your energy field! You must have experienced some differences between the energy states. Some typical descriptions of these energy states are listed below. See if you share any of these experiences.

Expanded: Heard more noises and sounds, became aware of movement and the vibrations of others, felt good, open, free, felt more vulnerable, and less focused.

Contracted: Very aware of body sounds and personal state of being, felt hemmed in and uncomfortable, felt safe, very intense feeling.

Normal: Very easy and comfortable, glad to be back to that state, more aware of usual sense of space.

What is particularly interesting is that every interaction we have with the world on a daily basis, naturally follows a similar pattern, but this has hitherto taken place unconsciously. Now try this:

While you are sitting, lower your eyes and look at your knees. As you are doing so, observe inwardly the shape and breadth of your energy and how it feels.

Now, look upward and outward and focus on something or somebody in the distance. Again, inwardly observe the shape and breadth of your energy and how it feels. Different? How?

You may wish to repeat this several times in different circumstances until you are really able to discern the difference between the energy states.

This sensation and feeling relates to how we experience our energy space. It is different with every place and person that we relate to. In fact, when we look up and out, our energy naturally expands and shares that space.

Now repeat this exercise, but this time do it inside your Cosmic Cross energy bubble and observe the difference.

It does make a difference when you have a more clearly defined sense of space and boundaries. What is also fantastic is that the when you are in your Cosmic Cross energy bubble, the awareness is not just of the boundary, but of the boundary in relation to your center! There is always a relationship between your inner and outer awareness. This is what makes this skill so important in psychic work as well as in managing your life.

The ability to expand and contract your energy field at will is a major psychic muscle builder, and a skill that has many uses, particularly when it comes to psychic cleansing and protection.

8

Cleansing and Protection

Cleansing and protection go hand-in-hand toward good personal energy management. The skills required are based on the principles that you have been introduced to in previous chapters. Energy management is the conscious use of energy skills to direct all your daily life circumstances, not just your allotted "spiritual time." It helps you to come back to yourself, to give yourself space and time for awareness, to make conscious life choices, to get your bearings, and to act more clearly.

Cleansing Your Energy Field

Just as we cleanse our physical body on a daily basis, so too do we need to cleanse our energy field, because this also accumulates grime in the form of stagnant energy from a variety of sources. The cleansing process does not take long to carry out and it has several benefits. On a short-term basis, it clears psychic energy stagnation from the system so that you feel lighter and better. On a long-term basis, it frees the circulation of your energy system and strengthens it. This gives you clarity of thought and a better capacity for energy storage and channeling. This is advantageous whether you are just going about your daily business or specifically doing psychic or healing work.

There are many methods of cleansing to choose from, and all begin with being centered. This starts by using the elements of energy control that you have already been introduced to—*Intention* plus *Imagination* plus *Breath*. In other words, set your intention as "cleansing" and use your imagination to visualize how that can be carried out according to your circumstances (see some suggestions below). Breathe in the appropriate rhythmic pattern to start the process.

Negativity and tension are the signs of stagnant mental and emotional energy that are held within the astral and etheric fields. This is also mirrored in the physical body in muscular tension, stress, and feeling "out of sorts."

Breathing is by far the most important and powerful technique to use in conjunction with visualization in cleansing. The goal is to stimulate the flow of life force through each field, causing it to expand and release the stagnation. This brings about greater balance and harmony within each body as well as between the physical and etheric parts of a body. Remember that the breath links the mind and body, the inner and outer worlds, and that the Yogic Vedas teach, "Mind follows breath as breath follows mind." This is simple, it costs nothing, and all that is required is that you *do* it consciously!

Some Cleansing Techniques
Choose a technique that suits the situation and time that you have at your disposal for performing the exercise. Most of these exercises can be done in a really short period of time as well as over more extended time periods. You must practice doing them both for long and short intervals while you are in a calm state of mind, then you should be able to recall the techniques when needed during stressful situations.

The Simplest Thing to Do—Breathing

Your intention (i.e. focus of concentration and sense of purpose) must be directed upon the breath that is moving through you and that is pushing out darkness and tension and drawing in light and vitality. Whether you sit for one minute, five minutes, or fifty minutes, this simple exercise cleanses you and refocuses your attention to your center. It brings peace. It is really useful to do in the middle or the end of a busy and stressful day. Take a minute alone and try it out.

Sit in a comfortable upright posture and activate your Cosmic Cross. Concentrate on the physical sensation of the flow of breath *gently* in through the nostrils and down into the lungs. Hold your breath comfortably being aware of the sensation of vitality that you are extracting from the air and drawing into your body cells. Exhale slowly and gently and pause for a comfortable amount of time, feeling peaceful, refreshed, and cleansed. Do this in a rhythmic manner and watch how the phases within the cycle of breathing become longer. Be aware of your energy state. When you are ready to "come back," stop the structured breathing, wriggle your fingers and toes, raise your arms above your head, stretch, lower your arms, and open your eyes.

Smile—Another Simple Thing to Cleanse

Never underestimate the power of a smile! The corners of the mouth are linked to a portion of the brain that controls the release of natural mood-producing chemicals into the brain and blood. Smiling lifts your mood and your spirit. It helps you to breathe more deeply and rhythmically and "come back to yourself." Frowning is a symptom of worry, but it can also cause worry. Too much thinking and analyzing makes you up-tight physically, emotionally, and mentally. Smiling and laughing free your solar plexus (refer to the chakra section to remind you). This reverses any negativity that is stored there. Even faking a smile does the job! Just lift the corners of your mouth a little bit three times, then grin and flash your teeth for a few moments and observe what happens. Then, take a deep breath in, and while smiling, stretch upwards and "tickle" the sky with your fingertips. As you exhale, lower your arms and keep smiling. Then proceed with your day.

Fountain Cleansing Breath
Do the short version, which is a minimum of three complete breaths or do it for five minutes and really charge yourself up. You can do it anywhere. This is a good preamble for healing work or to do at the beginning or end of your day.

Sit comfortably in an upright position with your feet flat on the floor and your hands resting on your knees.

Breath one: As you inhale, visualize a fountain of bright light bubbling upward from the earth, through your body, to above your head. Hold and feel the light breaking up and loosening your energies. Exhale and imagine the water droplets pouring outward and downward toward the earth, circulating energy. Pause and allow this image to continue.

Breath two: Inhale again and, as the water bubbles upward, imagine all darkness and stagnation in the energy field being gathered upward within the bubbling water droplets. Hold your breath and allow this to continue. Exhale, and experience all darkness and negativity being carried downward, to be absorbed into the earth and neutralized. Pause and continue to feel the process.

Breath Three: Repeat this again at least one more time, or until you feel light and clear.

When you have finished, raise your arms above your head, stretch, lower your arms, and open your eyes.

Draining Stagnation and Filling With Light

For the purposes of psychic work, it is important to have an understanding of these concepts and to be clear about what your intentions are before using these terms in visualization processes. Light and darkness are key metaphorical concepts used within psychic and spiritual work.

The light of the sun supplies us with the source of energy that makes life on earth possible, and sunlight makes it possible to see the outer world clearly. It traditionally represents the spiritual world, the active, positive, outgoing optimistic state of mind, and the energized state of being. Darkness represents mystery, the unknown and unseen, and the inner world—and it engenders fear. For this reason it can represent negativity and evil (live spelled backward).

Another way of looking at darkness is to see it as being receptive and absorbing. If life is movement, then death means extinguishing the light and turning it into darkness. In the context of this exercise, light means flow of life force, and darkness represents a stagnant life force. If the life force does not flow within the energy bodies properly, then those areas are denied nourishment. This affects not only the energy field but also the physical plane below and the spiritual plane above. If life is the integrated flow of energy from the spiritual into the physical world and back again, we need to encourage this flow by using the tools at our disposal, which are thought forms and breathing techniques.

Sit in a comfortable, upright posture with your feet flat on the floor and your hands resting on your knees.

Activate your Cosmic Cross. At the head and foot ends of the vertical shaft within your Cosmic Cross, imagine porthole like hatches. Place your attention beneath your feet and open the bottom hatch. Inhale and imagine all the darkness, stagnation, and negativity in your energy field gathering into the central shaft. This continues as you hold the breath. As you exhale, feel it draining out through the bottom hatch into the earth where it will be neutralized.

Continue until you really can feel the sensation of this negative energy draining away and allow it to continue automatically on your exhalation and pause phases on its own.

Now focus your attention on the hatch above your head. Inhale and imagine cosmic healing light pouring through the head-hatch. Inhale the light, pause, and allow that light and life-force to flow into your field and to push all darkness and stagnation toward the center. Now exhale and drain the negative energies toward the bottom-hatch and into the earth. Allow this process to continue as you pause. Keep breathing in light and breathing out darkness. Imagine you are pouring out the darkness and filling with light. When you feel that the stagnation and darkness is cleared, close the bottom hatch first and bring in some more light until you are completely filled with it. Then close the top hatch and breathe some more, consciously circulating the new energy to within your energy egg. Relax your breathing and observe your state of being. When you have finished, raise your arms above your head, stretch, lower your arms, and open your eyes.

This can take a variable amount of time depending on how clogged up you are. However, you can do it anywhere you happen to be seated quietly for a few minutes.

White Light Visualization

Use this when you really want to clear yourself, or to clear another person or an atmosphere. Your goal is to burn away the dross. This technique is generated from within yourself, so you will need to bring your energy back to a normal state when you finish. It does take a while to do properly, so leave thirty minutes to complete it and to recover.

Sit in a comfortable upright posture with your feet flat on the floor and your hands resting on your knees, and activate your Cosmic Cross. Focus your attention in the heart and solar plexus centers. Imagine a ball of bright, white, fiery light. Imagine that with each breath, it grows and gathers life force, glowing and expanding progressively outward to fill first your physical body, then your etheric field, then your astral field, and then the room. Its bright fiery light burns all negativity and darkness in its path and you can feel yourself tingle with energy as you shine with cosmic light. When you feel sufficiently cleansed, imagine with every inward breath you are drawing the light emanation inward. Imagine that you are decreasing its shine until the ball that you have generated is just gently glowing within and awaiting future activation. When you have finished, raise your arms above your head, stretch, lower your arms, and open your eyes.

You will need to take a few minutes to reintegrate back into the real world once again. Drink some water and be quiet for a little while.

Using the Elements for Cleansing

We are made up of the four elements of fire, earth, air, and water. Each element contains certain attributes that are associated with physical, mental, emotional, and spiritual functions. If you are into such things as astrology, you may be aware of the meanings of these elements, but you may not have considered them in the way that we do spiritual purposes.

By using one or more of the elements, you can drain out stagnant energy as well as charge your energy field or that of other people. Think of what you lack and what you have too much of, then balance these by using the opposite element. For example, if you are "up in the *air*" and cannot make a decision, you should "*earth* yourself" and thus become practical and do something concrete immediately.

If you are doing healing work, think not only of cleansing yourself before and after, and of keeping the energy moving by breathing during this process, but also consider the balance of elements in your physical environment. Look at the function of the room and decide which element needs to dominate. You may also think of foods relating to the elements, so you may wish to experiment with your diet.

The following is a list of suggestions that you may wish to add to your techniques over time and to perform, visualize, or to have in your environment.

Earth: Gardening, tending houseplants, hugging a tree, lying on the floor, lying flat on the earth, walking barefoot on the ground, carpentry, crafts, and cooking. Imagine yourself as a tree and feel your feet rooted to the earth while extending your arms as branches with vital greenness into the sky. You may try slow sports, or eat green vegetables and seeds, nuts, or grains. Wear or look at the color green.

Water: Wash yourself in running water, swim, enjoy water sports, soak in a tub then stay in it while the water drains out. You may listen to music, make music, be creative, and cup your hands three to five inches apart around a stream of running tap water and feel the draining and charging of the energy exchange. Alternately, eat fruits or watery vegetables, fish, and liquids. Wear or look at the color blue.

Fire: Burn incense and candles, sunbathe, stare at a fire, or meditate on a candle flame. Perhaps engage in vigorous sports where running is involved. Cup hands three to five inches around a candle flame and exchange energies with it. Eat a lot of red meat, sugar, or spicy foods. Wear or look at the color red.

Air: Communicate, write, read, meditate, and contemplate, do puzzles and crosswords, breathe, open windows, stand in the wind and blow the cobwebs away, throw away old or useless things, and eat poultry or game birds. Wear or look at the color yellow.

The application of the knowledge of the elements is a key to understanding the foundations of many Western and Eastern Mystery traditions such as astrology, Tarot, Feng Shui, Chinese astrology, and much more.

Energy Protection
Are you a psychic sponge who picks up on everyone else's energies? Do you feel invaded by other people? Do you sometimes feel that you are too influenced by the negativity of others? If so, you may feel that you need some psychic protection. What most people want from protection is a decreased sensitivity to the vibrations of others or being able to avoid absorbing or identifying with others' energy states.

Whether you are going about your daily business or intend to perform any kind of psychic or healing work, you may find yourself picking up unnerving or unpleasant emotions from other people. Once you have picked up a negative emotion of this kind, it can take a while for it to disperse.

The most effective way to protect yourself is through *centeredness*. The way to achieve this is by activating—or blocking—your Cosmic Cross.

You may automatically think that protection means putting up walls or barriers of some sort, and this will make you safe. Unfortunately, you have to build walls and then maintain them constantly in order for them to work. This requires a great deal of energy output and attention. It is hard work to create walls, but it is easy work to consciously center yourself. Once you are in that centered state of being, you have the *space* to evaluate and the capacity to *perceive* the situation for what it is, and you can then *choose* how to deal with it rather than react to it. You do not have to take on the negativity that is thrown your way. You can sort what is theirs from what is yours. Centeredness creates an inner attitude and illustrates a difference between identifying with and resonating with negativity. In the context of healing, it also means that you refuse on an inner level to take on and carry around the "stuff " that belongs to others. You will know on a psychic level that it is not yours—and that it is does not make you a better person or healer to carry it. Therefore, in most life situations, creating a psychic barrier is not required.

When an actual barrier is needed as a stronger protective measure, what works best is creating images of mirrored or reflective surfaces. Any negativity that comes your way is reflected off the surface without it being aimed at anyone in particular. The mirror surface protects you from absorbing negative rays, but it requires energy and concentration to maintain. It can therefore be only short-lived. Mirrors and other sorts of barriers are also isolating, because they tend to cut out positive vibrations as well.

It is also imperative to remember proper ethics so that you never set out to harm another individual or to seek revenge. All actions will bounce back to the sender eventually, so take care what you send out. Your sole purpose must be to shield or protect yourself. These are powerful techniques that can be used for good or for evil purposes. So be careful and responsible in the way that you use them.

These barriers have to be created on the astral plane as strong thought forms. As always, when working on the astral plane, we use our "intention" and "imagination" to create the protective shield and we use our breathing to activate it.

There are many images that one can use to suit different circumstances as well as suiting each person's individual temperament. These can help you to create a protective space at speed if necessary. They vary in the breadth of space they provide around you as well as in their density. You need to choose the one that is most appropriate for the moment. It is, therefore, very important that you take the time to practice these methods a number of times when you are in a calm atmosphere. Then, if you find yourself in a situation where you might need to use the technique in an emergency, you will be able to remember it and you will have the confidence to use it. These methods work, believe me!

There are times when you may feel out of your depth when dealing with these matters. If you believe that you or someone you know is under serious psychic attack, it is best to consult someone who knows what they are doing. They will help by ritually putting up a mirror barrier around the appropriate person. In all cases of psychic attack, it is important to think about why the victim has attracted this problem. Then you can try to eliminate the possibility of it recurring by doing something about the inner attitude that created it in the first place. This is often the hardest part for the victim to come to terms with—that he may have some part in having attracted the situation. A trained and experienced psychic will know how to handle this.

Protection Visualizations

Some examples that you will need to practice using are listed below. They should not take long to set up or to take down. You should practice each type of visualization several times. Try these ideas out first when sitting and then standing, so that you will be comfortable doing them under any circumstances whenever the need arises.

Sit comfortably in an upright position with your feet flat on the floor and your hands resting on your knees. Activate your Cosmic Cross. Now try the following:

Make the skin of your energy bubble silvered like a mirror. Focus your attention on the membrane of your energy bubble. Imagine that a silver mirror finish is forming over it that is only reflective on the outside. This creates a kind of one-way mirror you can see out of but that no one else can penetrate. Once it is fully formed, concentrate on holding the image while observing your state of being.

This is a good way of isolating yourself from others because it cuts out all external stimuli and communication. It also gives you personal space.

Make the membrane of your energy bubble become thicker and ensure that it contains some reflective glitter. Do this using your imagination and breath until you feel muffled but not cut off. The reflective specks of glitter that are embedded within the thickened membrane will act to deflect any negativity that is coming your way.

Being thick-skinned allows you to be more hidden and protected from the vibrations of others, but it does not cut you off completely from communicating with them. This is good to use in meetings or in potentially contentious situations because you can create your own safe space.

Create a shiny metallic shield. Put the barrier up to protect a particular area or space. This is a functional visualization because shields and protection already go together in our subconscious mind. You can mentally hold the shield close to or away from your body.

Create a metallic wall between you and someone. Close your eyes and imagine it blocking them out. Make it big and thick or made of any shiny metal that you choose.

Do experiment with different ideas, because each metal has different inherent qualities. See if you can tell the difference between the different types.

A suit of armor. Do you need to stand your ground when you go into battle? Try mentally putting on a suit of armor that covers you completely and see what that feels like.

A flowing silver cloak. Do you feel like hiding? Whip on a complete cover-up cloak, like a burkah, in a black-silver shade. Not only will you disappear but you will bounce the energies of others off as well.

A silver lamé cat-suit or a superhero costume. Be swift and slinky in this form-fitting protection. This one is useful at close quarters, such as in elevators or trains at rush hour.

Anything else your imagination can conjure up. Notice the images that work with your subconscious mind to create a known structure for your energy field to work with. Come up with some more images that speak to you personally and try them out.

Withdrawing From the Influence of Others
In the previous chapter during our work on boundaries, we mentioned that the natural act of looking downward draws your attention inward while looking up draws your attention outward. Looking outward focuses your attention on an object or person and it initiates an energetic relationship. An energy link is naturally established with every person with whom we come into contact during the course of our day. This is the moment of connection. The deeper our involvement, the more hooked up we are with their energy field. These connections can unconsciously drain our energies and allow the other person's energies to leak into our field. It

is therefore useful to consciously disconnect at least once a day to bring our own energies back to ourselves. This connection also happens with objects and places that we become attached to. These exercises are useful for protection, in the sense that you reaffirm your boundaries (in addition to cleansing), so that you keep your energies clear.

Connect/Disconnect Exercises.
Activate your Cosmic Cross. Focus your attention in your heart and solar plexus centers and begin to breathe slowly, deeply, and rhythmically. Imagine that all the people with whom you have contacts and relationships are connected to you through wires extending from your heart and solar plexus areas. See these wires coming out of these centers going out into space and connecting with them. You should now consciously draw these wires back to your center. Using your breath as a pump, begin to draw them back to your center. Imagine that they unplug themselves and slide back like the automatic rewind on a vacuum cleaner cord or one of those tape measures that workmen use. Perhaps see this as a light ray that was connecting you and that is now disconnecting and coming back toward you.

Continue to breathe and draw only your energies back to your center and circulate them through your energy field. Eventually, you will feel that you are finished. Continue to breathe with awareness and observe your state of being. See if this feels different.

You ought to feel more solid and energetic. Do not worry that this will drive away your relationships forever! You can re-establish the link very easily—you just "plug in"! This is a wonderful cleansing exercise that is useful to do at the end of each day. It is particularly good if you work with a lot of people or work in a therapeutic capacity where you have a deep energy contact with others.

Clearing Your Field of the Influence of Others

It is useful to do this exercise with someone you know so that you can discuss it together afterward.

Sit across from someone. Close your eyes and become aware of your own energy space. Activate your Cosmic Cross. Look downward, open your eyes slightly, and be aware of your energy. Now, look up and out at that person, and observe the flow of your energy toward him. Be aware of the moment when a subtle connection is made, and notice any changes that occur in your awareness. Now close your eyes and maintain the energy connection by continuing to hold your head in an upright position.

When you wish to withdraw from the person's field, start to gather your own energies together in a cloud of light. Using your breath as a pump, draw the cloud that contains only your own energies back toward your energy field. When you are aware that there is nothing more to pull back, you will feel the moment of disconnection. Continue to breathe slowly to reintegrate and circulate the energies around your field. Breathe normally and observe your state of being. When you are ready to come back, take a deep breath in, stretch, exhale, and open your eyes.

Ask your friend whether he experienced anything and then share your experience with him. You both may be surprised to find you experienced similar as well as different things.

This exercise is designed to sensitize you and to make you aware of the energy interactions that occur between people—in particular, the *beginning, middle,* and *end* of each of these. Obviously you cannot apply this on a daily basis because it takes time and concentration. However, you can bring this experience into positive use during the course of your daily interactions with people.

The beginning: Be aware that you are connecting when you enter into any relationship with others.

The middle: You are sharing subtle information through that contact, so be aware of it and value whatever comes from that part of your self, manifesting in sensation, emotion, ideas, and images. These are the impressions that you draw upon within the course of contact and communication with other people. This can be an amazing asset to have at your disposal.

The end: Know that when it is time to end the contact because you must do more than simply walk away and close the door. You must draw your energies back into yourself. Setting your intention, taking a few deep breaths while drawing back your light, and unplugging will make a huge difference in your life. It will help you to be more present in your next interaction with the next person who comes along, and also to avoid carrying anybody else's energies around with you.

Cleansing Your Energy from Objects

Objects hold an energy charge that is inherent to their structure. They also absorb their owner's energy charge. This is why psychometry works. This is also why it is important to ritually cleanse objects, in order to neutralize the object's field. Try this with different objects and compare your results. This exercise puts you in touch with the object but is not meant to completely cleanse the object per se—although it will withdraw your energies from it.

Sit across from an interesting object. Close your eyes and become aware of your own energy space. Activate your Cosmic Cross. Look downward, open your eyes slightly, and be aware of your energy. Now look up and outward to the object, and observe the flow of your energy. Be aware of a subtle connection and of any changes in your awareness.

Now look downward again and be aware of any change in your energies. Repeat this several times. The last time you look down, close your eyes and imagine that any of *your own* energies that remain within that object's field are gathering together in a cloud of light. Then, as you breathe, pull them back towards your solar plexus center.

When you are aware that there is nothing more to pull back, breathe slowly and circulate the energies around your field. Breathe normally and observe your state of being. When ready, take a deep breath in, stretch, exhale, and open your eyes. Evaluate your experience.

Withdrawing Your Energy From Places
Places have an inherent energy. Natural sites are influenced by the geologic structures, topographic contours, and the dominance of other elements present. Buildings concentrate and influence the natural energies of the site. In addition, they contain inherent qualities in construction and design that influence how energies flow within them, thus influencing the people who use them. Feng Shui, geomancy, and geopathic stress are some of the relevant areas you may wish to look into for more information relating to this principle.

To heighten your awareness of the influence of the energy of places, try doing the following exercise in a variety of locations; for example, in the countryside, in an urban area, in different buildings or rooms.

Sit comfortably in your chosen place with your feet flat on the ground, your hands in your lap, and your eyes closed. Activate your Cosmic Cross and observe your state of being. Now breathe and expand your bubble outward in all directions to the desired distance. Fill the room, the house, or your chosen area.

Now that you have filled the space, continue to breathe and enter into an energetic relationship with that place. Be conscious of absorbing the energetic atmosphere. Be aware of any changes in sensation, emotion, image, or thought that you may have while you are in that space.

When you are ready to disconnect, take several conscious breaths and begin to draw back the intensity of your focus on the place. Begin to consciously contract your energy field back to its normal shape, with each breath concentrating your energies back into your "self" and leaving behind the energies that belong to the place. Once this is done, sit and breathe normally for a while and review your experiences. When you are ready to come back, take a deep breath, hold it and stretch, exhale, and open your eyes.

This covers the basic principles of cleansing and protection. I cannot emphasize how important it is to practice these techniques from time to time so that you can open your inner "toolbox" and make an appropriate choice of method.

9

Interpretation Skills

Practice Makes Perfect

Once you have inner information from a dream or a meditation, the next step is to learn how to interpret it and to express it with confidence. This is a skill that takes a lot of practice. It is a good idea to join a group at some point and to study psychic development with others, because they will often receive similar information, and sharing this can help to spark off memories and help you to build your confidence. The more you express your inner perceptions and have them validated, the more confident you will become in the truth of your perceptions and in sharing them with others.

The way to approach interpretation is basically the same, whether we receive information out of the blue, ask inner questions, or use external tools for divination.

Look at the overall message.
Analyze the individual elements.
Identify any repeating patterns.
Relate them to something particular—such as an event, a
    person or an inner state and/or the question that
    you asked in the first place.
Put all the elements back together again.

Look at the overall message.

Simple messages arrive as a very strong feeling or a specific image.

Complex messages may come to you as a long dream with different scenes within a guided meditation with plenty of information to process, or as a series of images relating to a person or an object.

Do You Think It Is a Literal or Symbolic Message?

Literal messages are usually straightforward. They take place as if in present time and they are often logical.

Symbolic messages are usually filled with images mixed from different times and places in your life and they can be quite strange. They resemble dreams, where you see people and places from your past in situations and places that you recognize from your present life.

Think about the messages that you have received in the past. Have they been literal or symbolic? This will show the way you will receive messages in the future, because the way that these are transmitted to you and received by you depends upon your psychic structure.

When you mentally repeat the message or read through it in your notes, try not to prejudge its meaning; look at it as a whole.

Out of the Blue

If you receive an inner message that comes from nowhere, you need to consider what you were doing when you received that message. It is likely to relate to the moment and to be an insight about the past or to something coming up in the near future. Remember that the way you perceive the message will depend on your individual psychic strengths. You will need to take a risk in order to confirm the validity of the perception by checking it.

Example:

A student called Jane told me the following story: She was walking down a street toward home, thinking of nothing in particular other than what to make for dinner. As she turned the corner, she had a fleeting image of her mother, accompanied by a feeling of shock—and this passed quickly. She did not think too much about it as she still had a way to go and several errands to do before arriving home.

When she got home, on an impulse she decided to call her mother. Her sister answered the phone, saying that she was just about to call to let her know that mother had a fall and was in the emergency room waiting to be x-rayed. Jane had the image and the feeling, but she did not know the context of her perception. Calling on an "impulse" confirmed her fleeting psychic message, which she had received as an emotionally charged thought form.

This is a pretty straightforward message with no difficult interpretation required, just the willingness to confirm its validity. Many of these types of message are fairly literal and it is not until they are confirmed, that you will know what they mean.

Dreams

We all dream, whether we can remember them or not: it is a necessary physiological function. Think of dreaming as moving your primary awareness from the physical world to your inner world. Your subconscious mind will most frequently rise to the inner astral level in your dream, according to your own psychic structure. I put dreaming in three categories for interpretation purposes: psychological dreams, premonitions, and astral travel. Here is a clue to beginning to understand interpretation of your inner world.

Psychological dreams are characterized by being absurd and surreal combinations of time, place, and people. Everything in this level of dreaming needs to be deciphered, as it is highly symbolic and everyone in the dream is a part of you.

Daydreams are moments when you let go of logical thinking and let your mind and imagination drift. These are often times when fragments of information make themselves known to you.

Premonitions occur most often in dream states or in meditation rather than in daydreams. Some people have frequent premonitions. What is significant about them is that they are always literal and never symbolic! What is happening makes sense, it is sequential, and it seems real. What is difficult about premonitions is that you only get a fragment of information rather than being able to see it within a larger context. This makes it hard to know when or within what context it will happen. People who regularly have premonitions can usually identify a pattern of manifestation. In other words, there is a particular interval between the time of the premonition and moment of the event.

Dreams can also be about people or places you are not familiar with. You may see a plane crash and burn, hear the screams, etc. However, you will not be able to predict where, when, or how it will happen, only that it will happen and you will be able to identify it when it does.

Astral travel is a state in which your total inner awareness is focused at a high level of the astral plane. You have a lucid state of consciousness so that you act and function fully in logical time within the astral plane. Although this can be developed as an independent conscious psychic function in a meditative capacity, it also happens in the dream state.

Interpreting Meditations

I call meditation conscious dreaming. This means that you remain conscious as you go into your inner world and come out with insight, inspiration, and information. As psychic development is all about going within in a methodical manner and with awareness, it is inevitable that much of what you need to do is to find a way to make sense out of the messages that your inner world gives you.

There are different goals to meditative practice. As intention is the key to structuring entry into your inner world, the goal of the meditation will determine the level you seek to aim. This can be from aspiring to "no mind" or God consciousness, to seeking information and insight for yourself or others. If you go within to the level of the astral where the information is held, then you will need to find a way of interpreting the images and associated thoughts, feelings, and sensations you receive.

Guided meditations are constructed to take you to specific inner places where you can purposefully retrieve information that you have perceived and stored but that are not able to look at consciously. This provides a format for interpreting your inner experiences.

Asking Inner Questions

Personal meditations in which you seek information are structured through your intention. Asking inner questions is a very important part of this process, because they determine not only the answer that you receive, but also how you will go about approaching the interpretation. The question provides structure for your inner self so that it can attract answers, and this always needs to be referred back to. It is therefore really important to ask clear and precise questions, using words that have meaning to you.

When doing psychic investigations, I often ask lots of inner questions as well as set up inner image models in order to retrieve chunks of information that I know my client will want to hear about. Any information that I receive will be interpreted according to the question that is being asked.

When formulating inner questions avoid vague words or phrases such as, "Is it good for me?" "Are they nice?" "Is this the right person for me?" You can only use words like *good, nice,* and *right* if you know exactly what they mean to you.

Ask questions that elicit responses that are descriptive, such as, "What is the way forward with regard to work?" "What does the new house the person will be moving to look like?"

When asking yes/no questions, the question needs to be framed in such a way that the answer is yes or no. "Will he keep the same job?" "Will she be moving house within the next six months?"

A Sample Using Yes/No or Descriptive Questions to Elicit Inner Information

Q. Will Jane be moving in the next 6 months? *Yes.*

Q. Will it be this month? *Mentally name the month and you will get a yes or no response.*

Q. What will Jane's new house look like? *I see a house with white wooden slats and brick. I see a porch. It will have a small overgrown front garden and lots of trees around it. It will be on a busy street—and so on.*

Learning to formulate clear inner questions will also be useful to you when learning other kinds of divination techniques such as card reading or I Ching.

Pattern Reading—Story Telling

Much of the work involved in giving effective readings in addition to interpreting inner information is through pattern reading. This means observing what is repeated in the images, thoughts, or feelings that you receive. Sometimes this means recognizing that particular symbols have specific meanings for you and starting to identify them consciously. For instance, a flower could signify an anniversary or a peace offering, a book could denote knowledge or information, rubbish bags could show that it is time to have a clear out.

You should also observe repetitions of colors, people, or places that you know and so on. Whether it is symbolic or literal, the repeated pattern will become an important part of the way that you interpret the information.

Telling a story means taking the different elements within it and linking them together in a logical flow of information. There is nothing more frustrating than receiving bits of information without any context to which to apply them.

Symbolism

Images in dreams and meditations can take on symbolic significance. They may mean more than their simple appearance. This is because they are selected by your subconscious mind to convey a meaning for you to decipher. As stated above, you need to refer to your unique life experiences to understand your personal symbolism rather than rely upon stock interpretations.

What is also interesting is that, although many of the events, places, objects, or even people within your meditations or dreams refer to the past, they usually relate to circumstances happening in the present. They can represent inner states and parts of you rather than the person or place that is shown to you. This is a difficult concept to apply if you are not used to it.

Objects and places often relate to significant times or events in your past experiences. Houses represent the different parts of your life; landscapes represent different inner natural states; the weather represents your emotional life, i.e. cloudy, rainy, sunny and so forth; and objects contain sentimental significance.

People can symbolize a part of you rather than just individuals in your dreams. Male, female, young, old, innocent, dark and frightening, faceless or known—they are all aspects of yourself that you can meet and get to know. If you are meditating on someone in particular, then everything you receive about that person, including other names or information regarding other people in their life, is literal. If you are meditating on inner guides or helpers, they can be either symbolic or actual inner plane helpers. It can sometimes be difficult to discern whether these images are literal or symbolic. It is helpful to look at the context of how the information appears.

Language and metaphor is important, so words that you choose to describe your inner experiences become significant. After all, you chose particular words for reason. Look for double meanings and puns, look for patterns associated with images, or colors that repeat themselves within the imagery.

Color offers information about the inner emotional states with a dream or a meditation. This is so whether they appear as a color in the environment, as a geometric pattern, as clothing, or as decor. See the chapter on color interpretation to figure out the precise meaning that this has for you.

Sensations—Emotional and Physical

When I give a reading, the first thing I do is to center myself and observe my state of being—physically, emotionally, and mentally. When I intentionally connect to my client, I note changes in sensations, emotions, thoughts, and images and I know that what I perceive of these belongs to him and not to me. The pulse and rhythm of their energies are different to mine.

I have found that the movement of inner energy on a feeling level provides physical and emotional information, whether for someone else or for myself. Naturally, if you are asking specifically about either yourself or about someone else, it is clear to whom the information pertains. If you are uncertain whether it is about someone else or yourself, then you have to withdraw your energies from the other person and observe your own state of being. Once you have done this, you can expand them once again so as to share in the client's energies and see if the sensation repeats itself. If it does—then your impression is confirmed. Otherwise, ask some specific inner questions about the client in order to glean more information.

Emotional Feelings

Any perceived emotion such as anger, joy, frustration, depression, coolness, enthusiasm, fear, and so on, needs to be linked to an image, thought, or situation to which you can mentally connect.

Example:
Victoria is sitting alone with her eyes closed, in her front room, relaxing and listening to music after a hard day's work, which has been made all the harder due to a good deal of political upheaval at the office. She is not thinking of anything in particular and suddenly sees an image of an orange cat—and she feels fear.

Interpretation:
Elements that can be analyzed, that Victoria cannot link to any particular thought process.

> **Orange:** Politics, negotiation, group energy.
> **Cat:** Animals generally relate to the instinctive side of human nature. Cats are independent creatures that are also emotionally sensitive. As it happens, Victoria does not like cats and she does not trust them.
> **Fear:** Literal emotion. Upon reflection, Victoria felt the fear predominantly in her solar plexus area. The solar plexus governs decision-making and action.

Victoria receives an inner message that she feels fearful about current internal office politics. She does not like someone who is involved, and she is very sensitive to the atmosphere. She needs to remain aloof from the situation and not react to anything without thinking it through.

Directionality
Emotions drive us to use our energies. If you close your eyes and tune in to someone, look to the balance of energies within their auric space. Observe the direction of sensation within your own body. Image-linked movement will indicate the following:

Right: Relates to doing, activity, worldly life; that which you show to others.

Left: Relates to personal life, inner space, leisure time and receptivity.

Center: Relates to the self, consciousness; what is happening now.

Forward: Relates to the future, the impulse of how the individual feels about his progress, and his motivation.

Back: Relates to the past, deeper psychological states, old issues; that which blocks their progress.

Sample Interpretation

Julia came to see me for a reading, and when I tune in to her energies, I become aware of heaviness in my heart center, accompanied by an emotional sadness. In addition, I was aware of a dark gray-blue color. I then focus on the astral field and note that the right side is tighter and more held in. There is a distinct nervous energy with a forward and back pulse to it. On the left side, the field is more expanded and very busy with lots of colors swirling about.

What I tell her is: (*Heart center*) You are experiencing a lot of sadness right now, along with negative feelings about yourself and your inability to believe you can have what you desire emotionally within your relationships. (*Right side*) In your outer life you feel inhibited and constrained by outer circumstances (*tight and held in*). You feel very nervous, and you feel as if you are taking two steps forward and one step backward and reacting to others rather than being able to take initiative (*forward back pulse*). (*Left side*) On a personal level, you are spending a lot of time considering your situation (*expanded*) and are very emotional (*lots of colors*). You are not able to express that (*swirling movement*).

Physical Signs give information about the person's health and their physical or their emotional state. For instance, coldness can be poor circulation or fear, depending on the context in which you receive that information.

> **Surface sensations:** Tingling, itching, heat, cold, gooseflesh, shivering.
> **Tastes:** Bitter, sour, sweet, spicy, metallic, specific flavors.
> **Smells:** Floral, green, sour.
> **Actions:** Restlessness, twitching, heaviness.
> **Pain in the body:** Joints, organs.

Remember that there is always more information that will come through than simply the sensations you feel. The sensations must be interpreted in association with an image or in relation to another person's experience of life.

Inner Image Models
In order to get a quick answer, I structure the way I receive information by creating an image model. This provides a built-in structural template upon which my astral databank can pin information. The beauty of this is that it conforms to the way we naturally process information. It is quick, accurate and everyone can do it easily—unless they intervene by thinking! It is a really good way to practice interpretation skills because it is formulaic.

Boxes are a natural organizational form of image; one of my favorites is the Four World Box.

SPIRITUAL
MENTAL
EMOTIONAL
PHYSICAL

When I tune into these categories on behalf of a client, the level or levels that are affected will light up in my mind's eye. Once this happens, I can then proceed to ask more questions of my higher self in order to delve more deeply into the matter that I need to investigate. I can set up as many boxes as I like and look at the levels of connection between people.

Energy Eggs
I visualize others as being contained within their own Cosmic Cross energy egg. I can see their chakras like traffic lights and the colors indicate what is going on within that individual.

Trees
As a living energy, trees make wonderful meditation structures, representing our physical body, the landscape, and environment in which they grow. Whether a tree is alone or among other plants, it exists in different states of maturity, and each species of tree has unique qualities associated with it. We are all familiar with many trees, so it is not hard for our subconscious minds to select the appropriate image message. Try the following, keeping a pen and paper handy.

Close your eyes and relax, breathing deeply and rhythmically. Now ask your inner self to see yourself as a tree. This will reflect where you are now in your life. Continue to relax and be open, look at the screen that lies before your mind's eye and observe the scene. It should not take long. Once the image has presented itself, tell yourself to remember it in detail, then take a deep breath in, raise your arms above your head, exhale, lower your arms, and open your eyes. Write down and/or draw what you saw. Do not forget to make note of the atmosphere, landscape, weather, time of day, any other plants around, colors, and anything else that appears.

How to Interpret This

The tree you see is you.

Other plants and trees around you represent others. Note their distance from you.

Is your tree a sapling, or is it mature?

What season is it going through?

Is it bearing leaves, flowers, fruits or seeds?

The landscape represents you, in your life, right now.

The time of day represents your inner or outer life.

The weather represents your internal emotional environment.

Sample Tree Meditation

I saw Megan as a silver birch, surrounded by pine trees in a forest. Around the birch tree, which was in the center of the picture, was a clear forest floor. The surrounding pines were dark green and thickly packed. The birch tree was graceful and tall, with many branches, but with a few yellow leaves left on it. It was midday wintertime, cold, sunny, and crisp.

What I Told Megan:

The references to my meditation vision are shown in brackets.

You are a sensitive, graceful, and mature person (*silver birch, tall and graceful*). The whole of you is exposed at the moment. (*I can see the whole tree, including the roots*). You provide the center for many others right now and they need you and depend on you (*surrounded by vigorous dark green pine trees*). You can preserve your own sense of space and center, even though others place their demands upon you. (*Center of picture, a clear space on the forest floor around the tree*). You maintain an optimistic (*sunny*) attitude. You are also in a gestational period of time though, so just allow things to keep going—finishing up the few ideas and projects that have been left over from the creative time that you have just come through (*wintertime, yellow— ideas and administration, leaves thoughts*).

As you can see, this image provides an amazing format for gathering a great deal of intimate information quickly and easily. It is useful in assessing other people when you do not have much actual information about them. This is because your inner self notices things that you will not let your outer self acknowledge! Try this with people you know well, and share what you get and your interpretation with them to see if there is confirmation of your perceptions.

Flowers
These are a simpler aspect of nature than trees that can be used as an image model, and the interpretation method is similar. Look at the stage of the plant, the color of the flower, shape or stem, leaves, and the bloom.

Houses
These also make great metaphorical image models because they come in so many architectural styles. They are set in a landscape; each room will represent an area in a person's life; and they can be in varying states of repair. They are constructs, and as such, they represent what we have constructed for ourselves in our life.

10

Understanding Color

We have seen through the course of this book that color plays an important role in how we perceive, understand, and store information. It is really difficult to describe a color. This is why we often use references to the physical and natural world to communicate what a color looks like, because they act as a point of common experience. Some common examples are grass green, forest green, blood red, battleship gray, sky blue, sunflower yellow, and so on.

In addition to the shared meanings of colors, you will have personal associations with each shade of color, depending upon your life experiences. All interpretations of color must take your experience into consideration, because the color has been selected specifically from your astral databank to represent a particular energy state and a personalized symbol.

Color and the Aura

The astral body of the aura stores information as color. The colors represent qualities of energy that are applied to different areas of life experience. We bring all our life experiences to bear upon each moment of our life. Our auras therefore reflect this as color. Some colors change rapidly, while others stay the same throughout life.

If you can see auras, then an understanding of color will help you to understand what you are seeing. If you cannot see auras with your eyes open, then there are other ways in which to perceive aura energy colors on an inner level. In either case, before you can begin to interpret auras, you must become aware of colors and their meaning and influence.

The Meanings of Colors

This is a big subject that you may feel it is hard to get to grips with. However, I believe that your daily experience in your outer and your inner life means that you know a lot more than you realize.

There are many sayings in our language referring to states of consciousness and color. You may never have given thought to the origin of these sayings. They relate to a specific color that generated by the state of consciousness that is described within the astral field of the individual.

Here are some examples of these sayings.

He is *"yellow"* (cowardly):	Pale yellow mixed with gray
She was *red* with rage:	Crimson red with angular black lines running through
He is in a *brown* study:	Dark blue brown
She was *green* with envy:	Lime green
I am feeling *blue:*	Grey medium blue
I am in the *pink* of health:	A pink glow
That's *peachy!*	Medium peach orange

Shades of Color are Shades of Meaning

The colors that cannot be reduced to any other color (primary colors) are red, yellow, and blue. If you mix any two of these primary colors, you get the secondary colors. Red with yellow is orange, yellow with blue is green, and blue plus red is purple. These are the bright colors. For the purpose of understanding the meanings of the colors, it is easiest to relate to the bright color that represents the foundation meaning of the color.

Mixing the bright color with either black or white produces varying shades, each of which carries a different meaning. The tone of a color represents its value, and the shade represents the depth of color.

Black	Bright Color	White

Mixing the bright color with black suppresses the expression of the color, or makes it earthier.

Mixing the bright color with white dilutes the power of expression, making it softer and eventually more ethereal.

Colors in themselves are neither "good" nor "bad." They are expressions of energy and nothing more. It could be said that "brights" mixed with black are "negative," which may be construed as being "bad." This is a misleading interpretation. It is often necessary and appropriate to suppress or withhold energy, or to make it more focused within the earth plane.

For example, if someone has difficulty in expressing their sexuality, then dark reds are very good at helping them. Conversely, colors that are mixed with white are not necessarily more spiritual just because they are more ethereal. A very pale color can mean that the persona may be very wishy-washy or noncommittal, which may not be appropriate behavior.

Color interpretation is a subtle skill that takes time to master. Learning how you have internalized the meanings of colors and becoming more confident in your understanding is the first step. You can do many things to expand your awareness of what colors mean. Some useful exercises are provided below.

Color diary

Make a color reference book for yourself. This will help you to become aware of your experiences and associations with colors. Using a loose-leaf binder, dedicate one section to each color. This way you can add pages to each section over time. Collect color samples of fabrics, pictures of colors in nature, etc. and jot down your interpretations. Make a word list of color associations for physical, emotional, mental, and spiritual levels of meaning for each color. Using a set of watercolors, start with bright color at center of a horizontal sheet and mix colors progressively to the left, using black until you reach black and to the right using white until you reach white. Do this for every color. Think of each shade of color and go within to find your experience of the color.

To understand the symbolism of secondary colors, think about combining the key meaning of the two primary colors.

SHADES OF RED		
BRIGHT	Scarlet, crimson, etc.	Oxygenated blood, inflammation, fever, rash, temper, rage, irritated, irritable, passionate, sexual, energetic, hurried, chilies, tomatoes, red peppers, strawberries.
PINK	Rose, sugary	Healthy blood supply, rosy, innocent, feminine, blushing, girly, guava, baby girls.
DARK	Maroon, plum, deep cherry	Masculine, earthy, sensual, hidden motives, paprika, leather.

Listed in the "Bright Color Meanings" table are the basic concepts associated with each color. These can stimulate you to add your own associations to the list.

Color and Your Psychic Self

There are many ways color can be used within psychic development work. It can be used as a tool for understanding within the context of interpreting what you get within dreams. It can also be utilized in a meditative context when asking questions or as a tool for stimulating and expanding your energies and changing your world.

Below are some exercises for you to experiment with. Remember to record your experiences and reflect upon them.

Color Sensitization Exercises

Meditate on an individual color in all its shades. Use your color diary and lay out the material you have collected, and refresh your memory by reading it and looking at the pictures. Close your eyes and breathe deeply and rhythmically; visualize the color and silently sound its name within your own mind. Allow all your associations to float into your awareness. Do not try to control the thoughts that arise, just observe them. You may be aware of music coming to mind, feeling, sensation, or smell associations starting to arise. Tell yourself that you will recall them when you return to waking consciousness. Stay in this state for as long as you wish. Then write down your experiences.

BRIGHT COLOR MEANINGS		
WHITE	Purity	All colors manifest simultaneously. Allows other colors to be set off against it and is neutral in this sense. Blandness, reflective can act as a barrier by suggesting purity and detachment.
BLACK	Mystery	All color non-manifest. Withdrawn, silent, absorbing, detaching, lacking life force, dead.
GRAY	Hiding	Fearful, uneasy, withdrawn, neutral, bland, smoke screen.
RED	Stimulating	Active, passionate, physical, energetic, aggressive, assertive, sexual, outgoing, impulsive, volatile, angry, hot, irritated/irritable, feverish.
PINK	Gentle	Sentimental, loving, romantic, vulnerable, healthy.
ORANGE	Social	Ambition, appetite, warm, organizing, mentally creative, inquisitive, political, negotiator, self-opinionated, proud.
YELLOW	Intellectual	Intellect, joy, optimism, harmonizing, liveliness, rationality, attentive to detail, clear thinking, discriminating, judgmental.
GREEN	Nurturing	Balanced, nature loving, practical, naïve, empathic, jealous, difficulty setting boundaries, over responsible, smothering.
TURQUOISE	Expansive	Expressive, *avant-garde*, risk taking, networking, travel, exotic, freedom, restless, initiating energy, interest in language.
BLUE	Devotion	Piety, peace loving, loyal, detached, melancholic, sympathy, sensitive, receptive, reserved, stubborn, strong opinions, cautious, creative, focused.
INDIGO	Intensity	Idealistic, sincerity, deep thinking & feeling, reserved, loner tendency, rigid.
VIOLET	Spiritual	Religious devotion, magical, compelling, magnetic, mystical, otherworldly, hermetic, sincere, intense, fanatical, separated.
PURPLE	Pomp	Mystery, arrogance, theatrical, ambition for power.
BROWN	Material	Combination of any three colors. Fixed, earthy, insecure, materialistic.

Saturate your open-eye vision with a particular color.
Choose a color and find a physical sample, such
as a scarf, a cushion, or a large piece of colored
paper for this exercise. You might even find the
color in nature or as part of some decor. Sit at a
distance from the colored object and relax your
physical body. Close your eyes; activate your
cosmic cross and observe your state of being.
Open your eyes comfortably wide and gaze with
your eyes unfocused. As you inhale, imagine
drawing that color into you, saturating your
energy field with its nature. Absorb it and exhale.
Continue until you have had enough. Close your eyes
relax your breathing and observe your state of
being. What has changed? What did you notice
physically, emotionally, and mentally about
yourself when in contact with that color? Write it
down.

Color Breathing as a Variation From the Previous Exercise

Visualize a colored cloud around you and breathe it in,
absorbing it fully into your energy field. Instead
of gazing at the color externally, generate the
color from your imagination. Sit comfortably,
activate your Cosmic Cross and observe your
state of being. All around your head, imagine a
cloud of the chosen color enveloping you. Inhale
the color and see it streaming into your nostrils
and descending into your lungs. Hold the breath
and allow the color to be absorbed by your
energy field.
Exhale and push the color deeper into your body.
Pause—and then begin the cycle again until you are full
of the color. Then stop the visualization and allow
yourself to observe your state of being, noting

any changes within you in response to having "ingested" the color. Open your eyes, return to waking consciousness, and write down your experiences.

Color Sensing with Hands

It is not only your eyes that are sensitive to color and light, but also your skin. Try this and see if you can detect differences in how colors feel.

Lay out sheets of different colored art paper on a table. With your eyes closed, hover your hands over the colored sheets of paper and be open to any differing sensations.

Open your eyes to verify what you have felt. Remember the energy exercises that I described earlier in this book, because you may experience this as tingling, temperature, magnetism and so on. These sensations will be subtle—but you may surprise yourself!

Color in Meditations and Dreams

In order to address how to interpret colors within the context of dreams and meditations you have to:

Know what the color means.

Look for colors that repeat in the context of your inner experience.

Think about how the color gives insight into the "story," based on how and where it shows up within the context of the inner experience.

Remember that colors represent psychological and physical states that are intimately linked to emotions. Colors can appear in landscape, decor, clothing, or atmosphere. The way they show up can be so varied.

Remember that your inner mind selected them purposefully to convey information, so they must be viewed within this context.

Other Practical Applications

Color not only represents particular psychophysical states, but it also influences the energetic environment. Begin to be aware of how you can use color to change how you feel about yourself in addition to the way that it will influence how other people interact with you. This relates to psychic work in that your increased awareness can begin to make a concrete positive impact upon your life and on the lives of others. Send out more conscious messages about yourself by applying your understanding of color. Here are some exercises to try out to increase your awareness.

Color Preferences

Sit, relax, and close your eyes. Imagine yourself standing in front of your closet. Imagine that you are reaching out. Open your closet doors and begin to look through the clothes that are hanging on the rail.

What is the dominant color of the clothes?
Are there any colors missing?
Are the colors different for day or evening wear, work or
        leisurewear?

Now go to your chest of drawers and look through them, noting the above questions. When you have done this, ask your inner self, "What does this say about me?" Observe the answer. When you are ready, take a deep breath, raise your arms above your head, stretch and exhale, then lower your arms and open your eyes. Write down your observations and impressions.

What did you learn about yourself regarding the colors that you prefer to wear and those you do not? Look back at the color list provided and think about what those colors mean to you. Are there any colors you do not like to wear? It may appear in the environment around you. If you do not like a color at all, this means you are not in touch with the positive aspects of that specific energy in your life. It would be good to do to some of the sensitization exercises listed above and see if this changes your perspective and understanding.

Purposeful Color Dressing

What do you do when you go for an interview or go on a date or when you want to create an impression on others? Appropriate style is important, but color is more important because it sets up a psychological energy field around you that has an unconscious impact upon the observer. Experiment with what you know about color to create impressions and see if it makes a difference in how people see you and relate to you.

Some Simple Examples

Fade into neutrality: Wear gray or pastel shades.
Be a bold presence: Wear a bright shade or black
                          and white.

Be in control: Wear darker colors.
Be cool: Wear cool blue/white tones.
Be warm: Wear red, orange and yellow
        with black.

Remember to make notes of your observations.

Decor

Alter the energy of your environment by using color. Consider the function of the room and what you want to do when in it. Choose the color and the shade accordingly.

When considering sales, marketing, and advertising, think about what you do and choose the color it represents it as a profession, then project it in your literature, business cards, and so on.

This is the beginning of an adventure with color; have fun! There are many other applications of color, such as auras and healing, that are beyond the scope of this book.

11

Some Advanced Energy Techniques

Once you begin to feel comfortable and familiar with the basics covered in this book, you may wish to stretch yourself and try these very effective meditations.

About Energy Withdrawal Exercises

In previous chapters, you learned how to separate yourself from other people's energies on a face-to-face basis. There are several other ways that you can separate your own energy from that of others, either generally or specifically. These serve both cleansing and protective functions. They are cleansing because they allow you to clarify and consolidate your own energy; they are protective in that your energy field will become more contained and condensed. The two methods described below are useful in different ways, and they can be carried out without the person or people in question being present. This is important, because often in the process of relating to others, we pick up all sorts of messages from them that we are not actually aware of during contact. We also tend to spread our energy out in lots of different directions and leave unfinished, unresolved business in place that may distort future contact with that person or with others.

The first method is excellent for drawing your energies back in on a general basis. If you have not been able to "end" or "close off" contacts throughout your day, this general withdrawal exercise will be useful. You can do this exercise as often as you wish.

Drawing Your Energies Back to Yourself

Sit in a comfortable, upright position, feet flat on the floor, hands in your lap and relax. Activate your Cosmic Cross. Focus your attention on your heart and solar plexus centers and breathe slowly, deeply, and rhythmically.

Imagine that all the people with whom you have relationships are connected to you through wires or rays of light that extend from your heart and solar plexus areas. Become aware of these centers going out into space and connecting to others.

Using your breath as a pump, begin to draw or wind these lines back towards your center. Imagine that the wires unplug themselves and slide back like the cord rewind on a vacuum cleaner, or that the rays of light are retreating back into you. As you breathe, know that you are drawing only your own energies back. Feel your energy return to your center and circulate; reintegrate these lines back into your field. Be aware that you feel more solid and energetic. When you have finished, you will experience the sense that there is nothing more to pull in. Breathe and be aware of your state of being.

Prepare yourself to come back, take a deep breath, raise your arms above your head and stretch, lower your arms, exhale, and open your eyes.

The next exercise is complex; it is also very powerful. It may help you to resolve relationships that are troubling you. The trouble may be occurring now or it may have occurred in the past. The person or group of people can be alive or deceased, and not present in your life at all at the time that you carry out the exercise. This is because you will be dealing with the memory of the relationship rather than the actual person or people themselves.

The whole exercise takes place within your astral field, and it helps you to draw back the projected energy that you have invested in the "other," to take responsibility for your own actions within the relationship and it ultimately neutralizes the negative thought-form that is carried within your astral body via the chakras.

You may have heard of "cutting the ties" from others. I have found this leaves traces behind in the astral, and it does not always neutralize the situation properly. I have discovered that the next exercise is far more effective in changing the energetic nature of the aura, and therefore, the attitude and approach of the individual towards the person or people in question.

Amazing things frequently happen. If the person is still alive, but you have not heard from them in years, they will get in touch with you or you will hear from them. This is because the energy links between you have persisted on a subconscious basis.

What is so wonderful is that if and when you speak with them or see them, your attitude toward them will be different; what really bothered you about them no longer seems to be a trigger for negative emotions.

There are several important technical matters that you must consider before embarking upon this exercise:

This is not an exercise to be done on a daily basis. Your aura will need time in which to integrate the results, and this takes several days. Once a week should be sufficient for this exercise.

Give yourself enough uninterrupted time in which to carry out the exercise. You do not want to leave yourself up in the air during this one.

You may find that it is not possible to draw back a particular chakra's energy completely during the course of the exercise. This is because you are not ready to let go. I advise you to continue with the next chakra, and then to return to the problem chakra. You may then find it easier to draw it back to you. If not, proceed to the next stage of sending away, etc. and know that you will need to repeat the whole process with reference to that person at a future date, until such time as you can completely release them.

Choose the person from whom you wish to separate before you start the meditation. This person may be alive, dead, in your past, or in your present life. If this involves your present life and you know that you will see her again, that is fine. This exercise helps to give clarity to your relationship. It is designed to resolve your own problems with the person, and this will have a positive effect on your relationship. It is designed to give you the option of reconnecting with her if your relationship needs further exploration, and thus of maintaining contact with her.

Keep breathing and stay focused. It can be easy to drift off during the exercise. If that happens, proceed from where you remember that you were, breathe, and concentrate on the process once again, staying focused on breath and visualization.

Observe carefully. You will notice that as you pull your energies back from the other person, it is not unusual to experience flashes of sensory memory of your relationship. You will also notice that some chakra connections are stronger than others, which helps you to have a better understanding of the nature of the relationship.

Conscious Separation From Others for Unresolved Problems With Others at the Astral Level

Sit in a comfortable, upright position, feet flat on the floor, hands in your lap, and relax your physical body. Close your eyes; breathe and activate your Cosmic Cross.

Place your attention in the center of your Cross and see a small version of yourself resting in that place, but surrounded by an energy bubble. As you breathe, see the bubble containing "you" begin to rise slowly upward along the vertical shaft, up through the heart center, continuing slowly upward through the throat center, through the third eye and up through the crown center, until you emerge though the crown center. Begin to float slowly downward in front of you within your bubble, until the "you" image reaches eye level and floats over to the left side, at eye level and within visual range.

Now, see a bubble containing the person you have chosen to separate from, floating toward you. It settles in front of you, to the right side at eye level.

Allow your little bubble to face the person in their
  bubble; then ask to be shown your energy links to
  that person through your chakras. Observe them.
You are now going to change your position, so bring the
  bubble containing the little "you" around in front
  of you, facing forward, and position the other
  person's bubble to face you. Focus your attention
  in your root center, unplug the line from the other
  person, and begin to draw in your energy
  connection from their root center back to
  yourself. Using your breath as a pump, remember
  to draw only your own energies back from the
  other person into yourself. Breathe and stay with
  the process, observing it carefully. When you
  have drawn back all your energy projection from
  their root center, you will experience a sensation
  of release. Then, move your attention up to the
  sacral chakra and continue the same way,
  working progressively upward, chakra by chakra,
  toward the crown center, completing the process
  of reabsorbing only your own energies back into
  each of your chakras before moving on to the
  next one.
Take the time now to draw back your own energy from
  each chakra, starting at the root center and
  working upward to the crown center.
When you have completely disconnected your energy
  centers from this person, see the image of
  yourself floating back to the left field of your
  vision and the image of the other person floating
  to the right. Ask for both of you to be filled with
  cosmic light, and see this happen.
Watch the other person begin to float off out of your
  Energy Egg. Say goodbye to them and affirm that
  you release them, and that they will only reappear

in your life if necessary and according to God's will. Watch them float off into the distance.

When they are gone from your field, allow the image of you to move to the center of your field of vision, float upward and come to rest for a moment above your crown center. Now allow the image to descend into your crown center, see the image begin to expand progressively, so that this image of "you" in the bubble fits fully into your whole body and becomes integrated into your field.

Breathe, relax, and take a few moments to observe your state of being—physically, mentally, and emotionally. Reflect upon your experience.

When you are ready to return to waking consciousness, take a deep breath in, hold and stretch, exhale, open your eyes, lower your arms, and come back to waking consciousness.

About Chakra Healing Meditation

This advanced exercise can be carried out on a daily basis, and it can be done for five or fifty minutes, depending upon the time that you have available. This is a form of self-healing, cleansing, and centering. It incorporates most of the techniques covered in this book. Thus, it involves posture and breathing, visualization, knowledge of the chakras, and color symbolism in addition to the introduction of specific sounds to vibrate and stimulate the energy flows within the chakras.

Sound vibration also affects the mental plane structures, bringing alignment that affects the flow of energy down into the emotional and etheric/physical bodies. There are many different word-sound sequences as well as pitches that can be used in association with the chakras. In this exercise, just use these vowel sound combinations with any pitch that suits your voice or the way you are feeling at the time. Sound the word in your mind and allow it to grow within you. As you breathe out, carry the sound progressively outward, concentrating on vibrating the particular center that you are working on at the time. Try different pitches. Try varying the loudness and try holding the note for varying durations. Experiment and watch what happens.

Chakra Healing Meditation

Sit in a comfortable upright posture, feet flat on the floor, hands resting on your knees. Close your eyes; breathe slowly and deeply and activate your Cosmic Cross. Observe your state of being— physically, emotionally, and mentally.

Focus your attention on your root chakra. Wiggle your tailbone by flexing the muscles around the base of your spine. Begin to consciously breathe into the center, paying attention to each phase of breath and how it affects the chakra. Be aware of how the energy carried by the breath begins to circulate the energies within the chakra in every direction. As you breathe into the root chakra, begin to visualize the color red. See it being absorbed and circulated through the chakra, loosening up any blockages or stagnation. The sound "EH" is beginning to grow within you. As you exhale, allow the sound "EH" to emerge, vibrating that center.

Relax your breathing and observe your state of being.

Move your attention upward to the sacral chakra. Place your awareness in your pelvis and lower back and consciously breathe into the sacral center, paying attention to the effect of each phase of breath. Be aware of how the energy carried by the breath begins to circulate the energies within the chakra.

Visualize the color orange, continue to breathe into the sacral chakra, and see the color being absorbed and circulated through the chakra, loosening up any blockages or stagnation. The sound "OH" is beginning to grow within you. As you exhale, allow the sound "OH" to emerge, vibrating that center.

Move your attention upward to the solar plexus chakra. Place your awareness in your upper abdomen, just below the breastbone, and consciously breathe into the center, paying attention to the effect of each phase of breath. Be aware of how the energy carried by the breath begins to circulate the energies within the chakra. Visualizing the color yellow, continue to breathe into the solar plexus chakra, and see the color being absorbed and circulated through it, loosening up any blockages or stagnation. The sound "OOO" is beginning to grow within you. Inhale, and on the exhalation, allow the sound "OOO" to emerge, vibrating that center.

Relax your breathing and observe your state of being.

Move your attention upwards to the heart chakra. Place your awareness in your chest and middle back, and consciously breathe into your center, paying attention to the effect of each phase of breath. Be aware of how the energy carried by the breath begins to circulate the energies within the chakra. Visualizing the color green, continue to breathe into the heart chakra, and see the color being absorbed and circulated through it, loosening up any blockages or stagnation. The sound "AAA" is beginning to grow within you. As you exhale, allow the sound "AAA" to emerge, vibrating that center.

Relax your breathing and observe your state of being.

Move your attention upward to the throat chakra. Place your awareness in your throat and neck and consciously breathe into the center, paying attention to the effect of each phase of breath. Be aware of how the energy carried by the breath begins to circulate the energies within the chakra. Visualizing the color turquoise, continue to breathe into the throat chakra, and see the color being absorbed and circulated through it, loosening up any blockages or stagnation. The sound "EEYAHH" is beginning to grow within you. As you exhale, allow the sound "EEYAHH" to emerge, vibrating that center.

Relax your breathing and observe your state of being.

Move your attention upwards to the third eye chakra. Place your awareness in the space between your eyebrows and consciously breathe into the center, paying attention to the effect of each phase of breath. Be aware of how the energy carried by the breath begins to circulate the energies within the chakra. Visualizing the color indigo blue, continue to breathe into the third eye center, and see the color being absorbed and circulating through it, loosening up any blockages or stagnation. The sound "EEE" is beginning to grow within you. As you exhale, allow the sound "EEE" to emerge, vibrating that center.

Relax your breathing and observe your state of being.

Move your attention upward to the crown chakra. Place your awareness in the center of your brain and consciously breathe into the center, paying attention to the effect of each phase of breath. Be aware of how the energy carried by the breath begins to circulate the energies upwards within the chakra. Visualizing the color violet, continue to breathe into the third eye center, and see the

color being absorbed and circulating through it,
loosening up any blockages or stagnation. The
sound "AUM" is beginning to grow within you.
As you exhale, allow the sound "AUM" to
emerge, vibrating that center.
Relax your breathing and observe your state of being.
As you breathe, see all the colors of the chakras glow
within their centers. See and feel the colors
swirling around you in a cloud of light. Your
energy field is absorbing all it requires from the
spectrum of color, for your health and well-being
on every level—according to God's will.
Continue to breathe and receive.

It is finished. Prepare to come back to waking
consciousness refreshed, energized, and restored. Inhale.
Raise your arms above your head and stretch. Exhale,
lower your arms, and open your eyes, keeping that sense
of vitality and refreshment with you.

Finally...
Enjoy! Many of the meditations in this book—among
others—can be found on an educational CD, available
through www.foundathc.org.uk.

12

Conclusion

"The end is the beginning, for as one door closes, another opens."
This is a book about the foundations of practical psychic development. I continue to be amazed with the results that I get with my students, and I never tire of teaching the basics because there is always something new for me to learn. All psychic training is an elaboration of this basic work.

As I leave you to work your way through this book, I hope you will be inspired to try the exercises, to think about your inner world and how it is constructed. I hope that you will begin to open up to your inner world with a sense of greater control and confidence. I trust that you will gain insight into your true personality, into the way that you make decisions and into the way that you relate to yourself and others.

The door is open to a new world—and it is an exciting place that needs to be explored sensibly. Ask many questions, read, share—and above all, enjoy your practice. Make your inner life an integrated part of your daily life and I know that you will reap rewards.

Nina Ashby
September 2003

Appendix 1: Glossary

Astral: Greek; from *astra*, meaning star. The body that relates the personal body to the planetary body.

Aura: Sanskrit; air. The total of the different layers of the energy field. Often mistaken for the personality aspect of the astral body.

Centered: Axis, pivot, hub, midline or point to which things move or are drawn. Centeredness is a desirable state to strive for in psychic work. It means your attention is located more within than without, making it possible for you to be more insightful.

Control: To command; to regulate; to direct; to restrain. *Appropriate* control is something we all want to achieve over all aspects of our lives.

Energy: Life-force that exists at every vibrational frequency—electrical, solar, etc. This word is freely used within the context of personal development work, because we are seeking to understand the movement and transformations of life force within the human experience.

Observer: One who watches systematically. This is an important skill to develop because it enables you to change how you take action.

Patterns: An arrangement of forms or colors or a design. In psychic work, we look for patterns of behavior, which may be habits or patterns of meaning through repetitive images or thoughts.

Perception: To obtain knowledge through the senses. Psychic perception is the ability to gain knowledge through the extraphysical senses.

Power: The capacity for action.

Psychic: Derived from the Greek word *psyche*, meaning "pertaining to the soul, spirit, or mind." Psyche is the root of the words *psychic, psychology*, and *psychiatry*.

Psychology: The scientific study of the mind and its activities. Psychiatry is the study and treatment of mental disorders. Interesting! What is the relationship between the mind and the soul? Some formal approaches to understanding mind and behavior appear not to include the soul. Our psychic self therefore relates our soul to the pattern of our mind and spirit. Our psychic self stores our life experiences.

Querent: One who questions; the client, the person being read for by a professional psychic or other reader.

Soul: The spiritual and immortal part of human being; the seat of emotion, sentiment, and aspiration; the center of moral and intellectual powers; vigor; energy; the essence of moving spirit; a human being. The soul is an intelligence in which the sum total of all incarnation experiences is gathered. We only have limited access to all these experiences. Prior to incarnation, the soul identifies the areas that it seeks to perfect. Upon incarnation, a pattern is created for the individual that is reflected down the planes of manifestation. For example, the soul chooses the parents who provide the genetic structures and socio-economic conditions for the optimum growth of consciousness of the individual in this particular lifetime.

Spirit: Vital force; immortal part of man; God within.

Appendix 2: Psychic Reading Methods

Aura Reader: An aura reader is a clairvoyant who can specifically see the colors of the astral field while his eyes are open. He can interpret the meaning of the colors in relation to the physical, emotional and mental bodies.

Clairsentient: A clairsentient experiences sensations relating to physical states such as bodily health or earth energies. Astral smell, taste, and touch sensations are clairsentient phenomena. These are the "gut feeling" brigade.

Clairvoyant: One who tunes in to the astral body and sees images corresponding to thought forms generated by the individual. There is direct perception of the client's energy field. Clairvoyants usually work by looking within themselves, either with their eyes open or with their eyes closed. Clairvoyants are often good at dream interpretation because they are used to working with images and differentiating the levels from which they arise.

Direct Perception: Many psychics attune themselves to a person or a place in a direct way. In other words they experience directly within their own energy field the vibrations of the person or place in order to obtain information.

Empath: An empath uses his ability to tune into the emotions of others. Emotions are often read as movement, since emotions relate to *desire*, which fuels our activities. Empaths need to learn how to separate awareness of their own emotions from those of their clients.

Medium: Mediums use their psychic faculties, usually clairvoyance and clairaudience, to communicate with passed over souls and spirit intelligences. They act as a medium between the spirit and the client by transmitting information either by reporting what the spirit says or by directly channeling the message. Channeling occurs when the medium allows the spirit intelligence to enter into his own energy field and share its etheric body, enabling the spirit to speak directly via the medium's physical body both through gesture and voice. The medium also then shares the thoughts and emotions and any physical sensations that the passed over spirit intelligence wishes to convey.

Trance Mediums: These readers allow the depth of this etheric contact to occur either in a light trance state where they retain their own awareness to a great extent, or all the way to a deep trance state where they completely lose contact with their self-awareness and are almost completely taken over. Well-trained deep trance mediums learn how to work with their inner "intent" and with spirit guides who aid them to return from their deep trance states into normal waking consciousness.

Mental Intuitive: Mental intuitives perceive mental patterns. Information "drops into their minds." They receive mental impressions that are not primarily pictures or feelings. They do not hear other spirit voices; only their own voice in their head, telling them things.

Secondary Perception: This can be mediumship and/or the use of divination tools such as the ones listed below. These are the means through which they gain information that has to be translated and interpreted. In addition to using personal psychic sensitivity and skill, it is necessary to learn the technical structures and skills for each particular form of divination.

Divination

The following are the most common forms of divination, though other methods can be found around the world. Some, like astrology and palmistry, are more technical by nature and do not necessarily require psychic ability to carry them out, though a reasonable degree of intuition is very useful.

Astrology: This comprises the reading of the patterns of movement made by the stars and planets in relation to the earth. The astrologer creates a personal chart, which is made for the time when the client drew his first breath. It describes the client's earthly life, and it is a map of the patterns of his incarnating energies. It describes the soul's purpose, personality, parents, talents, and life events. It is an intellectual type of divination that requires a great deal of study and thought, and it demands a conceptual mind. It is my view that it is essential for all those who engage in spiritual work to have some knowledge of basic astrological principals.

Cards: This concerns a set of images representing different types of energy states—it is a kind of defined astral databank. Each card has a particular meaning in itself as well as within the context of the other cards drawn within the reading. Clients shuffle the array of energy-state images and allow the cards to magnetically rise to the top of the pack so they are selected and then spread out in a pattern. This pattern and the story that it tells are read back to the client. These days the Tarot is a popular form of card divination, but there are many others that can be used. Cards vary from having many image illustrations combined with words and numbers, to those that carry little more than words and numbers or to simple concept images that we see in playing cards. If you are good at working with images, cards may be the right avenue for you, and you would choose your preference from the many that are available today.

Color Readings: The reader interprets a series of colors that the client chooses. These might be color cards, ribbons, or any other colored object—including crystals, and these will be laid out in a predetermined format. A thorough knowledge of color correspondences and their associated psychological states is required.

Crystal Ball: This concerns the use of a natural or man-made lead crystal ball of any size, which acts as a focusing and amplifying instrument for the reader's clairvoyance. Quartz crystals have acknowledged resonant properties of electromagnetic amplification, and so these are used in radios and other forms of modern telecommunications, including computer chips. Not only does the reader benefit from heightened clairvoyance by this means, but he can also see actual patterns of clouds, smoke, and pathways within the crystal itself.

I Ching: This is an ancient Chinese form of divination, originally using four yarrow stalks and subsequently using coins. By asking a preformulated question, the querent throws the coins in a particular manner, and a pattern of yin and yang emerges. The hexagram that is formed is then looked up in the book of the I Ching Oracle, which answers the client's question. The answer is rarely straightforward—it is often enigmatic, requiring further contemplation.

Nature Readings: Flowers, sand, crystals, bones, shells etc. These forms of readings relate a great deal to the element that is used. The client needs first to ask a question, and then the pattern that emerges in colors, shapes, and placement will determine the outcome of the reading.

Palmistry: This relates to the reading of the hands' configuration, color, and lines. These elements reflect not only the physical health and constitution of the individual, but also his changing consciousness as the lines grow and change throughout his life. Aside from knowing the details of palmistry, much psychic information can also be gained by touching the client's hands during the course of the reading— and there are many working psychic palmists.

Psychometry: This relates to reading the energy contained within an object, so as to determine its history and its previous owner(s), or to act as a link with the client. The reader perceives the information via his own psychic strengths.

Runes: These are tiles that are inscribed with symbols representing different energy states. The querent selects individual tiles or a series of tiles. These are then laid out in a predetermined pattern and then interpreted by the reader in order to provide answers to questions.

Index